100 WORD SCRAMBLE

LARGE PRINT ACTIVITY BOOK

by Mablid Publishers

WRESTLING

BTUO   _ _ _ _

ROEP   _ _ _ _

STHTIEAN   _ _ _ _ _ _ _ _

PTOS   _ _ _ _

SLCFFUE   _ _ _ _ _ _ _

RYAADRVSE   _ _ _ _ _ _ _ _ _

CHIP   _ _ _ _

AESV   _ _ _ _

EVALT   _ _ _ _ _

ERLSTEEYF   _ _ _ _ _ _ _ _ _

NGRI   _ _ _ _

DNWO   _ _ _ _

Puzzle #2
BUNGEE JUMPING

WINSUMOPJGH   _ _ _ _ _ _ _ _ _ _ _

RUJPME   _ _ _ _ _ _

NEICDLU   _ _ _ _ _ _ _

NRNOTAPSOS   _ _ _ _ _ _ _ _ _ _

RARMONSTB   _ _ _ _ _ _ _ _ _

KYNAGHAM   _ _ _ _ _ _ _ _

EARH   _ _ _ _

SLOUE   _ _ _ _ _

PUNEOC   _ _ _ _ _ _

RPAROPATERO   _ _ _ _ _ _ _ _ _ _ _

HLMAA   _ _ _ _ _

AFLE   _ _ _ _

AEGER   _ _ _ _ _

RAAROTIDIIN   _ _ _ _ _ _ _ _ _ _ _

SRIAYOVNI   _ _ _ _ _ _ _ _ _

ERRIMP   _ _ _ _ _ _

ASREENGT   _ _ _ _ _ _ _ _

ISPEIDLC   _ _ _ _ _ _ _ _

KCOLB   _ _ _ _ _

HCCITEANNI   _ _ _ _ _ _ _ _ _ _

STPLIO   _ _ _ _ _ _

GEDBDAIR   _ _ _ _ _ _ _ _

UITBNLI   _ _ _ _ _ _ _

FITDR   _ _ _ _ _

Puzzle #4
SAVING MONEY

BCUL   _ _ _ _

ONUTIBFUL   _ _ _ _ _ _ _ _ _

SIGINNK   _ _ _ _ _ _ _

SREKTI   _ _ _ _ _ _

LBWO   _ _ _ _

TWIEH   _ _ _ _ _

DPRO   _ _ _ _

LSTA   _ _ _ _

ZRSGO   _ _ _ _ _

OPAMRSYNI   _ _ _ _ _ _ _ _ _

DORINE   _ _ _ _ _ _

DMRA   _ _ _ _

Puzzle #5
CALIFORNIA

NAAP   _ _ _ _

HACIBSL   _ _ _ _ _ _ _

AHDTAFE   _ _ _ _ _ _ _

CTJSKELAM   _ _ _ _ _ _ _ _ _

IADCLHPR   _ _ _ _ _ _ _

ONARAMPIS   _ _ _ _ _ _ _ _ _

CFAIL   _ _ _ _ _

OWOBOIBDNR _ _ _ _ _ _ _ _ _ _

WASTT   _ _ _ _ _

APUH   _ _ _ _

WIOKM   _ _ _ _ _

MYAO   _ _ _ _

Puzzle #6
SELF DEFENSE

TABAGRRG   _ _ _ _ _ _ _ _

HOANGTEP   _ _ _ _ _ _ _ _

NLTAFULTE   _ _ _ _ _ _ _ _ _

RREVOCE   _ _ _ _ _ _ _

EYBO   _ _ _ _

OFTR   _ _ _ _

UCRDPNTEOTE   _ _ _ _ _ _ _ _ _ _ _

IRTADAZME   _ _ _ _ _ _ _ _ _

ALRITIV   _ _ _ _ _ _ _

CNTOITNEN   _ _ _ _ _ _ _ _ _

SUOISLAYT   _ _ _ _ _ _ _ _ _

NIVTOIDINCA   _ _ _ _ _ _ _ _ _ _ _

Puzzle #7
PRESSURE COOKER

SPIULXNEO   _ _ _ _ _ _ _ _ _

ITLSRPEMSA   _ _ _ _ _ _ _ _ _ _

LGUBE   _ _ _ _ _

CMPITANH   _ _ _ _ _ _ _ _

RESSURPE   _ _ _ _ _ _ _ _

ZEGNEQSIU   _ _ _ _ _ _ _ _ _

RENDTIGA   _ _ _ _ _ _ _ _

FCIDALC   _ _ _ _ _ _ _

ILOPT   _ _ _ _ _

GYRINES   _ _ _ _ _ _ _

SRATT   _ _ _ _ _

ORBTIAV   _ _ _ _ _ _ _

Puzzle #8
POTTERY

OIALPDM   _ _ _ _ _ _ _

MALE   _ _ _ _

BURN   _ _ _ _

EALCD   _ _ _ _ _

YTPTOER   _ _ _ _ _ _ _

INEFACE   _ _ _ _ _ _ _

YACL   _ _ _ _

TNLIF   _ _ _ _ _

EFOSONT   _ _ _ _ _ _ _

RFUTAAEUMCN   _ _ _ _ _ _ _ _ _ _ _

MYAA   _ _ _ _

GEIARZL   _ _ _ _ _ _ _

Puzzle #9
WIND SURFING

KCRAN   _ _ _ _ _

OGOHTD   _ _ _ _ _ _

IOBNBB   _ _ _ _ _ _

AHLU   _ _ _ _

UAECRITNOT   _ _ _ _ _ _ _ _ _ _

RAEG   _ _ _ _

KKCI   _ _ _ _

ITDRF   _ _ _ _ _

TNEURSHO   _ _ _ _ _ _ _ _

PSRA   _ _ _ _

REOWCRSKC   _ _ _ _ _ _ _ _ _

GTUSY   _ _ _ _ _

Puzzle #10
PACKING LIST

SCTRIP   _ _ _ _ _ _

NOWD   _ _ _ _

KANR   _ _ _ _

CNEFLIT   _ _ _ _ _ _ _

EMRONTELN   _ _ _ _ _ _ _ _ _

AEMLM   _ _ _ _ _

AMEPHR   _ _ _ _ _ _

ENLCBAA   _ _ _ _ _ _ _

EOUSHLERC   _ _ _ _ _ _ _ _ _

LISO   _ _ _ _

TCRNIECU   _ _ _ _ _ _ _ _

EISMDED   _ _ _ _ _ _ _

Puzzle #11
WINE

UNPPETDA   _ _ _ _ _ _ _ _

BODDIE   _ _ _ _ _ _

HTRGEAIEM   _ _ _ _ _ _ _ _ _

SEPEAIXNV   _ _ _ _ _ _ _ _ _

RCOOEL   _ _ _ _ _ _

ACRLY   _ _ _ _ _

ELSE   _ _ _ _

TAPA   _ _ _ _

GSEDAO   _ _ _ _ _ _

AEARMDI   _ _ _ _ _ _ _

ALSBLBYU   _ _ _ _ _ _ _ _

STNIA   _ _ _ _ _

Puzzle #12
BUILDING

KHOO   _ _ _ _

REIP   _ _ _ _

EYVNIR   _ _ _ _ _ _

TNGAIES   _ _ _ _ _ _ _

HFSIUNR   _ _ _ _ _ _ _

RIROTEEX   _ _ _ _ _ _ _ _ _

ICANMAOHR   _ _ _ _ _ _ _ _ _ _

REEOLDM   _ _ _ _ _ _ _

RAREFT   _ _ _ _ _ _

TAECSL   _ _ _ _ _ _

DHFEEOLERR   _ _ _ _ _ _ _ _ _ _

ENRAANECYTW   _ _ _ _ _ _ _ _ _ _ _

COLLEGE SCHOLARSHIPS

NDHNOIS

_ _ _ _ _ _ _

OTRUT

_ _ _ _ _

TSFAF

_ _ _ _ _

MNMOOC

_ _ _ _ _ _

UAEEDTC

_ _ _ _ _ _ _

CYDAAEM

_ _ _ _ _ _ _

PEELX

_ _ _ _ _

LGAUETOCA

_ _ _ _ _ _ _ _ _

ENDAWR

_ _ _ _ _ _

RUTRICE

_ _ _ _ _ _ _

ATROHIRCLE

_ _ _ _ _ _ _ _ _ _

SHONUGI

_ _ _ _ _ _ _

Puzzle #14
PIZZA

OYODNB   _ _ _ _ _ _

EIWLEKIS   _ _ _ _ _ _ _ _

IUQLDSA   _ _ _ _ _ _ _

ARAVLOPP   _ _ _ _ _ _ _ _

OURCYT   _ _ _ _ _ _

ICHN   _ _ _ _

TRPEEHA   _ _ _ _ _ _ _

AMALORLEZZ   _ _ _ _ _ _ _ _ _ _

RIVAELABIN   _ _ _ _ _ _ _ _ _ _

VIELO   _ _ _ _ _

REONCEUN   _ _ _ _ _ _ _ _

RIDWE   _ _ _ _ _

Puzzle #15
SPECIAL OCCASIONS

HTORWEYNOT   _ _ _ _ _ _ _ _ _ _

UGNNICN   _ _ _ _ _ _ _

URIEMPM   _ _ _ _ _ _ _

RALME   _ _ _ _ _

HSPIOTLGT   _ _ _ _ _ _ _ _ _

TIFTENCO   _ _ _ _ _ _ _ _

PTOSTY   _ _ _ _ _ _

VERVE   _ _ _ _ _

ONPTI   _ _ _ _ _

SEUCRE   _ _ _ _ _ _

DRBROAOATRM   _ _ _ _ _ _ _ _ _ _ _

CSOHEN   _ _ _ _ _ _

Puzzle #16
MAPS

AETS   _ _ _ _

GSYMROCAHPO   _ _ _ _ _ _ _ _ _ _ _

NPOTRIICDE   _ _ _ _ _ _ _ _ _ _

HRAYD   _ _ _ _ _

ITITNYED   _ _ _ _ _ _ _ _

SIKKO   _ _ _ _ _

RIHPGCAS   _ _ _ _ _ _ _ _

EELFRI   _ _ _ _ _ _

TSAAL   _ _ _ _ _

WAHEERT   _ _ _ _ _ _ _

LPBREUISH   _ _ _ _ _ _ _ _ _

CSMSPAO   _ _ _ _ _ _ _

Puzzle #17
CLEANING SUPPLIES

TCESKRO

_ _ _ _ _ _ _

LTAARIEM

_ _ _ _ _ _ _ _

URPSREEAKMT

_ _ _ _ _ _ _ _ _ _ _

TUOBBMA

_ _ _ _ _ _ _

HAKNY

_ _ _ _ _

RMAWER

_ _ _ _ _ _

OBCM

_ _ _ _

ROAEFG

_ _ _ _ _ _

SEFL

_ _ _ _

LUIBT

_ _ _ _ _

REOCRG

_ _ _ _ _ _

ILANEGNSC

_ _ _ _ _ _ _ _ _

LMIF   _ _ _ _

IKCHT   _ _ _ _ _

TNTTAIA   _ _ _ _ _ _ _

ECVOR   _ _ _ _ _

MTTLEO   _ _ _ _ _ _

MIMSAA   _ _ _ _ _ _

BIUSNM   _ _ _ _ _ _

KMRU   _ _ _ _

AKNB   _ _ _ _

OVRE   _ _ _ _

NISSHENU   _ _ _ _ _ _ _ _

KDENRA   _ _ _ _ _ _

FUNNY

OPSFO

_ _ _ _ _

RAHC

_ _ _ _

IMIBTELLAIL

_ _ _ _ _ _ _ _ _ _

FDTA

_ _ _ _

TAYLS

_ _ _ _ _

ETVRERINER

_ _ _ _ _ _ _ _ _ _

WTIYT

_ _ _ _ _

NUGAYTH

_ _ _ _ _ _ _

NELVAE

_ _ _ _ _ _

UOOFBFN

_ _ _ _ _ _ _

HIAQNEURL

_ _ _ _ _ _ _ _ _

BECAICR

_ _ _ _ _ _ _

SHIRT

ISEKRPP   _ _ _ _ _ _ _

TKSCBLAIRH   _ _ _ _ _ _ _ _ _ _

RJASDTUE   _ _ _ _ _ _ _ _

MFNRLOAI   _ _ _ _ _ _ _ _

NATAFK   _ _ _ _ _ _

LATI   _ _ _ _

AMRONO   _ _ _ _ _ _

VDECINEE   _ _ _ _ _ _ _ _

BGYAG   _ _ _ _ _

UERTXTE   _ _ _ _ _ _ _

SAJPMYA   _ _ _ _ _ _ _

OTCNOT   _ _ _ _ _ _

Puzzle #21
BOUNDARIES

RILYALI   _ _ _ _ _ _ _

EURENIVS   _ _ _ _ _ _ _ _

NAOSHUTDLI   _ _ _ _ _ _ _ _ _ _

RARTATY   _ _ _ _ _ _ _

FSUOPSLUUER   _ _ _ _ _ _ _ _ _ _ _

HDYOYHARRPG   _ _ _ _ _ _ _ _ _ _ _

NCNNEIFDUO   _ _ _ _ _ _ _ _ _ _

NSEDSLOBU   _ _ _ _ _ _ _ _ _

TSGEEMN   _ _ _ _ _ _ _

TELDBMEAT   _ _ _ _ _ _ _ _ _

IUDSNNGO   _ _ _ _ _ _ _ _

UNIZADENGOR   _ _ _ _ _ _ _ _ _ _ _

Puzzle #22
MOBILE

EGTIBRKLZI   _ _ _ _ _ _ _ _ _ _

TAECNEO   _ _ _ _ _ _ _

MOLTEI   _ _ _ _ _ _

CHURN   _ _ _ _ _

XIELLFE   _ _ _ _ _ _ _

KOLEIBOMOB   _ _ _ _ _ _ _ _ _ _

GUETNO   _ _ _ _ _ _

OAMPARECGH   _ _ _ _ _ _ _ _ _ _

TTRHNESG   _ _ _ _ _ _ _ _

IGONRDEDD   _ _ _ _ _ _ _ _ _

RYLOTAUMAB   _ _ _ _ _ _ _ _ _ _

CENET   _ _ _ _ _

Puzzle #23
BUILDING A HOUSE

EPIEC   _ _ _ _ _

AGRRBUL   _ _ _ _ _ _ _

SACFUE   _ _ _ _ _ _

EBEUTOSLN   _ _ _ _ _ _ _ _ _

RTTERU   _ _ _ _ _ _

OEVLRTEA   _ _ _ _ _ _ _ _

LFTO   _ _ _ _

EAMRHTEGI   _ _ _ _ _ _ _ _ _

IOPCLY   _ _ _ _ _ _

OLSENTKE   _ _ _ _ _ _ _ _

KCED   _ _ _ _

ITRBATOA   _ _ _ _ _ _ _ _

Puzzle #24
WRITING POETRY

OEATVC _ _ _ _ _ _

MFLOASYU _ _ _ _ _ _ _ _

ETCTRE _ _ _ _ _ _

HCGIPAR _ _ _ _ _ _ _

TRASH _ _ _ _ _

KTSI _ _ _ _

MUVOOLSNIU _ _ _ _ _ _ _ _ _ _

YERL _ _ _ _

AOTRNE _ _ _ _ _ _

LBUL _ _ _ _

IRPERM _ _ _ _ _ _

ENTGUO _ _ _ _ _ _

Puzzle #25
PREGNANCY

TIAECNDC

_ _ _ _ _ _ _ _

TNNEOIEMNCF

_ _ _ _ _ _ _ _ _ _ _

CNENOITCOP

_ _ _ _ _ _ _ _ _ _

NMLTRUAAIR

_ _ _ _ _ _ _ _ _ _

CPERDSMEII

_ _ _ _ _ _ _ _ _ _

EOYYGOLCGN

_ _ _ _ _ _ _ _ _ _

HMPAIRDAG

_ _ _ _ _ _ _ _ _

OLRAB

_ _ _ _ _

NEMAALTR

_ _ _ _ _ _ _ _

QAUD

_ _ _ _

EIYHPERMSES

_ _ _ _ _ _ _ _ _ _ _

TYOOCFEPS

_ _ _ _ _ _ _ _ _

Puzzle #26
DOG

KINGWNO _ _ _ _ _ _ _

ANWF _ _ _ _

NERAY _ _ _ _ _

GFAL _ _ _ _

ECIPRH _ _ _ _ _ _

LAAAITSN _ _ _ _ _ _ _ _

RYROW _ _ _ _ _

RETROR _ _ _ _ _ _

ALENHDR _ _ _ _ _ _ _

AOUNIUTLL _ _ _ _ _ _ _ _ _

TBELKNA _ _ _ _ _ _ _

CTEHF _ _ _ _ _

Puzzle #27
RELIGION

STPMIAB _ _ _ _ _ _ _

MMLSIU _ _ _ _ _ _

OTNOIVED _ _ _ _ _ _ _ _

IROPZYSLEET _ _ _ _ _ _ _ _ _ _ _

FSLNIU _ _ _ _ _ _

AANTHP _ _ _ _ _ _

GIRLORNEII _ _ _ _ _ _ _ _ _ _

ASEPL _ _ _ _ _

IWENGKNAA _ _ _ _ _ _ _ _ _

HRMONAE _ _ _ _ _ _ _

EESHYR _ _ _ _ _ _

SATCONIM _ _ _ _ _ _ _ _

LAWK

_ _ _ _

WAFRD

_ _ _ _ _

IGTFED

_ _ _ _ _ _

IMCCO

_ _ _ _ _

TDLUA

_ _ _ _ _

ETRIFT

_ _ _ _ _ _

AMEBYOONG

_ _ _ _ _ _ _ _ _

FNSEULF

_ _ _ _ _ _ _

LCALGRIE

_ _ _ _ _ _ _ _

BUBBYL

_ _ _ _ _ _

EDPLIIAOPH

_ _ _ _ _ _ _ _ _ _

OTTIPE

_ _ _ _ _ _

Puzzle #29
BLOOD PRESSURE

ERHI   _ _ _ _

ARZIIAHBL   _ _ _ _ _ _ _ _ _

THOCRE   _ _ _ _ _ _

HTBMOIRSSO   _ _ _ _ _ _ _ _ _ _

OOLNES   _ _ _ _ _ _

SSTSIPAYHO   _ _ _ _ _ _ _ _ _ _

SMAHS   _ _ _ _ _

IURBME   _ _ _ _ _ _

RNHEAD   _ _ _ _ _ _

UVCAEEAT   _ _ _ _ _ _ _ _

ODLBYREBOR   _ _ _ _ _ _ _ _ _ _

ITODVOLARAS   _ _ _ _ _ _ _ _ _ _ _

Puzzle #30
PENNY STOCKS

TLAUIQDEI _ _ _ _ _ _ _ _ _

TENER _ _ _ _ _

UTATSCIIOF _ _ _ _ _ _ _ _ _ _

CTEEEHPREN _ _ _ _ _ _ _ _ _ _

TISKNLNFI _ _ _ _ _ _ _ _ _

SPAMT _ _ _ _ _

CSELO _ _ _ _ _

EEDERM _ _ _ _ _ _

OTORM _ _ _ _ _

OOBM _ _ _ _

ENVRTRDAUE _ _ _ _ _ _ _ _ _ _

ALRI _ _ _ _

ROMANTIC IDEAS

EPSPOO   _ _ _ _ _ _

ACIATTNFS   _ _ _ _ _ _ _ _ _

LAIISETD   _ _ _ _ _ _ _ _

ESEPSRX   _ _ _ _ _ _ _

LSCDEO   _ _ _ _ _ _

LUSUOIMN   _ _ _ _ _ _ _ _

FIHGLTY   _ _ _ _ _ _ _

ELSLNWPIRG   _ _ _ _ _ _ _ _ _ _

AEDYMR   _ _ _ _ _ _

SMDIELIA   _ _ _ _ _ _ _ _

EPSURIVO   _ _ _ _ _ _ _ _

LLCOAGI   _ _ _ _ _ _ _

Puzzle #32
TRAFFIC

TCAFOR　　　　　　_ _ _ _ _ _

NDBIONU　　　　　　_ _ _ _ _ _ _

OSTP　　　　　　_ _ _ _

EDLIY　　　　　　_ _ _ _ _

AEMK　　　　　　_ _ _ _

DMOLEUAT　　　　　　_ _ _ _ _ _ _ _

DOLEDTR　　　　　　_ _ _ _ _ _ _

HIRSOOB　　　　　　_ _ _ _ _ _ _

SYWPESXERA　　　　　　_ _ _ _ _ _ _ _ _ _

AAMTTGSIRE　　　　　　_ _ _ _ _ _ _ _ _ _

LOTOFLAF　　　　　　_ _ _ _ _ _ _ _

OITTNINTUIS　　　　　　_ _ _ _ _ _ _ _ _ _ _

Puzzle #33
SLOW DOWN

LYOG   _ _ _ _

UPLL   _ _ _ _

RTSRAE   _ _ _ _ _ _

TILO   _ _ _ _

NTNAEDA   _ _ _ _ _ _ _

AGFL   _ _ _ _

KSELA   _ _ _ _ _

IRFITEBUSL   _ _ _ _ _ _ _ _ _ _

ADHN   _ _ _ _

ADDWEL   _ _ _ _ _ _

TAABE   _ _ _ _ _

ALTSL   _ _ _ _ _

RBYED　　　　　　　_ _ _ _ _

KEPIS　　　　　　　_ _ _ _ _

AEPESKR　　　　　　_ _ _ _ _ _ _

CLFFIAOI　　　　　　_ _ _ _ _ _ _ _

XDFIE　　　　　　　_ _ _ _ _

AKAYK　　　　　　　_ _ _ _ _

XBSKOY　　　　　　_ _ _ _ _ _

DWOASH　　　　　　_ _ _ _ _ _

CORTNVE　　　　　　_ _ _ _ _ _ _

ACKJ　　　　　　　_ _ _ _

EODM　　　　　　　_ _ _ _

PUPQIELA　　　　　_ _ _ _ _ _ _ _

Puzzle #35
MAGIC

RSSETSNEEAN   _ _ _ _ _ _ _ _ _ _ _

ATAISMNL   _ _ _ _ _ _ _

IENEG   _ _ _ _ _

OEDRR   _ _ _ _ _

ELATUIERRT   _ _ _ _ _ _ _ _ _ _

UHIELM   _ _ _ _ _ _

CFOER   _ _ _ _ _

VLEAITET   _ _ _ _ _ _ _ _

RUCJNEO   _ _ _ _ _ _ _

CROJURNO   _ _ _ _ _ _ _ _

TELAHLC   _ _ _ _ _ _ _

ABDRACARAAB   _ _ _ _ _ _ _ _ _ _ _

Puzzle #36
PHOTOGRAPHY

RISETLB   _ _ _ _ _ _ _

BRCANGUDKO   _ _ _ _ _ _ _ _ _ _

UMHGOTS   _ _ _ _ _ _ _

RAODMKRO   _ _ _ _ _ _ _ _

ONRMEMOCHO   _ _ _ _ _ _ _ _ _ _

CIATCIN   _ _ _ _ _ _ _

ISIVNTESE   _ _ _ _ _ _ _ _ _

APOIGRRAHYD   _ _ _ _ _ _ _ _ _ _ _

CEROETARLCA   _ _ _ _ _ _ _ _ _ _ _

ESNSYZTIHE   _ _ _ _ _ _ _ _ _ _

INITTGS   _ _ _ _ _ _ _

GTOAURRVERO   _ _ _ _ _ _ _ _ _ _ _

MONEY

ADOTMEAOMCC   _ _ _ _ _ _ _ _ _ _ _

AEMBDRRESSA   _ _ _ _ _ _ _ _ _ _ _

LODE   _ _ _ _

RRIYE   _ _ _ _ _

BLUER   _ _ _ _ _

DIONEM   _ _ _ _ _ _

CPLAE   _ _ _ _ _

AENTRG   _ _ _ _ _ _

XDIFE   _ _ _ _ _

IDASLA   _ _ _ _ _ _

AHSL   _ _ _ _

EHINSR   _ _ _ _ _ _

Puzzle #38
TRAIN

ARLTTRE _ _ _ _ _ _ _

DORILARA _ _ _ _ _ _ _ _

AMOPRRG _ _ _ _ _ _ _

IGEUQPAE _ _ _ _ _ _ _ _

AKCB _ _ _ _

EVER _ _ _ _

LINEMSIOU _ _ _ _ _ _ _ _ _

ARTETCL _ _ _ _ _ _ _

RUIEN _ _ _ _ _

MCNETSEEAP _ _ _ _ _ _ _ _ _ _

GDAREN _ _ _ _ _ _

SACEL _ _ _ _ _

Puzzle #39
ARMY TRAINING

ITRTAITON   _ _ _ _ _ _ _ _ _

ISAEGGNED   _ _ _ _ _ _ _ _ _

DDNHKCAE   _ _ _ _ _ _ _ _

NRNAETUID   _ _ _ _ _ _ _ _ _

EMAEIHCZN   _ _ _ _ _ _ _ _ _

ODPDAKC   _ _ _ _ _ _ _

EGABGAG   _ _ _ _ _ _ _

CHAOCIGN   _ _ _ _ _ _ _ _

NCPSHIO   _ _ _ _ _ _ _

AJNAW   _ _ _ _ _

OTRES   _ _ _ _ _

EIPURCTDNAS   _ _ _ _ _ _ _ _ _ _ _

FRUIT

ENLDRYACREB   _ _ _ _ _ _ _ _ _ _ _

COMFIT   _ _ _ _ _ _

WPAAPW   _ _ _ _ _ _

ZQUEERSE   _ _ _ _ _ _ _ _

CNESLTNIGO   _ _ _ _ _ _ _ _ _ _

ELSO   _ _ _ _

UTUONIATFLC   _ _ _ _ _ _ _ _ _ _ _

IAFTRAA   _ _ _ _ _ _ _

RDOCNO   _ _ _ _ _ _

BOELDA   _ _ _ _ _ _

PPIAEGN   _ _ _ _ _ _ _

ECERPNRPOP   _ _ _ _ _ _ _ _ _ _

Puzzle #41
NOISE POLLUTION

RWLAB   _ _ _ _ _

UNSIQEETS   _ _ _ _ _ _ _ _ _

TCOUYR   _ _ _ _ _ _

PLONK   _ _ _ _ _

HPMUT   _ _ _ _ _

SFFELNU   _ _ _ _ _ _ _

HLCSA   _ _ _ _ _

OCPRTUINRO   _ _ _ _ _ _ _ _ _ _

NKISC   _ _ _ _ _

SINGOUND   _ _ _ _ _ _ _ _

WORC   _ _ _ _

BZZU   _ _ _ _

Puzzle #42
PACIFIC

RAWATA   _ _ _ _ _ _

AINLCEP   _ _ _ _ _ _ _

BILRAOBLD   _ _ _ _ _ _ _ _ _

OGOERN   _ _ _ _ _ _

NALGDCLAAUA   _ _ _ _ _ _ _ _ _ _ _

OOCK   _ _ _ _

AGMU   _ _ _ _

OHSAVDEHEL   _ _ _ _ _ _ _ _ _ _

UGSAR   _ _ _ _ _

GDHOFSI   _ _ _ _ _ _ _

HOOC   _ _ _ _

AIIHTT   _ _ _ _ _ _

Puzzle #43
CHILDHOOD MEMORIES

OIJRNU

_ _ _ _ _ _

HIRCEAV

_ _ _ _ _ _ _

KNIHIGTN

_ _ _ _ _ _ _ _

MIFR

_ _ _ _

SDIIICEALT

_ _ _ _ _ _ _ _ _ _

KFOL

_ _ _ _

LUTOEBR

_ _ _ _ _ _ _

TNCANCTOAEE

_ _ _ _ _ _ _ _ _ _ _

IEDEVRP

_ _ _ _ _ _ _

AEWKA

_ _ _ _ _

FUDRWLENO

_ _ _ _ _ _ _ _ _

INHKT

_ _ _ _ _

Puzzle #44
KIDS PODCASTS

ASSSEESR   _ _ _ _ _ _ _ _

GTEINREEC   _ _ _ _ _ _ _ _ _

RAWMS   _ _ _ _ _

OANNTW   _ _ _ _ _ _

UOLKOTO   _ _ _ _ _ _ _

CPLRLCEPAAW   _ _ _ _ _ _ _ _ _ _ _

OETTNANSOTI   _ _ _ _ _ _ _ _ _ _ _

VERURETO   _ _ _ _ _ _ _ _

BCEKIR   _ _ _ _ _ _

EDRLDTO   _ _ _ _ _ _ _

EGNRRA   _ _ _ _ _ _

AWEN   _ _ _ _

ABDYN   _ _ _ _ _

DYTEMIA   _ _ _ _ _ _ _

NEITWRZIE   _ _ _ _ _ _ _ _ _

PHTDE   _ _ _ _ _

ADDE   _ _ _ _

SOWN   _ _ _ _

HTCE   _ _ _ _

EGALZD   _ _ _ _ _ _

PORVA   _ _ _ _ _

ISOL   _ _ _ _

DANSOI   _ _ _ _ _ _

ERECNASYS   _ _ _ _ _ _ _ _ _

Puzzle #46
KOREA

ABEEFRCYC   _ _ _ _ _ _ _ _ _

OCECSNOISN   _ _ _ _ _ _ _ _ _ _

TIIWSRAE   _ _ _ _ _ _ _ _

HUMSATIS   _ _ _ _ _ _ _ _

YNGA   _ _ _ _

NHOC   _ _ _ _

UGATE   _ _ _ _ _

AEOKR   _ _ _ _ _

NAAPJ   _ _ _ _ _

TEUG   _ _ _ _

TRNEOILA   _ _ _ _ _ _ _ _

UMACTRAHR   _ _ _ _ _ _ _ _ _

Puzzle #47
BUG

GGLOEG   _ _ _ _ _ _

ATELSR   _ _ _ _ _ _

EOHNDR   _ _ _ _ _ _

HREPPOETER   _ _ _ _ _ _ _ _ _ _

GOELOUDDB   _ _ _ _ _ _ _ _ _

SPADCI   _ _ _ _ _ _

ERIFGBU   _ _ _ _ _ _ _

TILGBH   _ _ _ _ _ _

RCIEDO   _ _ _ _ _ _

NLEUIEQEVCA   _ _ _ _ _ _ _ _ _ _ _

HRATPNEIEM   _ _ _ _ _ _ _ _ _ _

EPST   _ _ _ _

Puzzle #48
SALES SKILLS

MIUAST   _ _ _ _ _ _

SICBA   _ _ _ _ _

ETHN   _ _ _ _

FNAKELR   _ _ _ _ _ _ _

GARINM   _ _ _ _ _ _

ECPA   _ _ _ _

YPKO   _ _ _ _

GLIHSUGS   _ _ _ _ _ _ _ _

EDSPE   _ _ _ _ _

DEAOHNEB   _ _ _ _ _ _ _ _

PPPREYE   _ _ _ _ _ _ _

NIRAGCH   _ _ _ _ _ _ _

Puzzle #49
VIOLIN LESSONS

NCHI   _ _ _ _

LCSSA   _ _ _ _ _

UETDE   _ _ _ _ _

NISG   _ _ _ _

OMNAIHRSC   _ _ _ _ _ _ _ _ _

ILNCCI   _ _ _ _ _ _

MRACAA   _ _ _ _ _ _

IRONDSO   _ _ _ _ _ _ _

SIOIINLVT   _ _ _ _ _ _ _ _ _

EWOBR   _ _ _ _ _

AEBRK   _ _ _ _ _

PSIPTNGO   _ _ _ _ _ _ _ _

UTOPUT   _ _ _ _ _ _

AELIACBMLP   _ _ _ _ _ _ _ _ _ _

GRAA   _ _ _ _

ALCOSELPD   _ _ _ _ _ _ _ _ _

OTEIYHCD   _ _ _ _ _ _ _ _

LFLUAEHTH   _ _ _ _ _ _ _ _ _

RTOTE   _ _ _ _ _

EEPSRUM   _ _ _ _ _ _ _

FTOS   _ _ _ _

RPEHYOBEL   _ _ _ _ _ _ _ _ _

FOMA   _ _ _ _

UARDCTS   _ _ _ _ _ _ _

CRAEF

_ _ _ _ _

RTSPO

_ _ _ _ _

AGHYEWIEHVT

_ _ _ _ _ _ _ _ _ _ _

OULF

_ _ _ _

KOPE

_ _ _ _

PLEOIRS

_ _ _ _ _ _ _

MSHLDEUIG

_ _ _ _ _ _ _ _ _

INONEOTNTC

_ _ _ _ _ _ _ _ _ _

EASQUR

_ _ _ _ _ _

JDGUE

_ _ _ _ _

TKEA

_ _ _ _

DAURG

_ _ _ _ _

Puzzle #52
HALLOWEEN

COMSTEU   _ _ _ _ _ _ _

AKMRRBBCA   _ _ _ _ _ _ _ _ _

TONCIDOIN   _ _ _ _ _ _ _ _ _

CTOREH   _ _ _ _ _ _

YNDCA   _ _ _ _ _

KETNOLSE   _ _ _ _ _ _ _ _

RRGFOAA   _ _ _ _ _ _ _

LPMEI   _ _ _ _ _

YIVIETTFS   _ _ _ _ _ _ _ _ _

PAOHOL   _ _ _ _ _ _

UGLY   _ _ _ _

HSAST   _ _ _ _ _

Puzzle #53
MAIL

BKLCRERBAY   _ _ _ _ _ _ _ _ _ _

FRMUFEL   _ _ _ _ _ _ _

TNCTMHAEAT   _ _ _ _ _ _ _ _ _ _

PHPRSOE   _ _ _ _ _ _ _

OEEHLNPOGI   _ _ _ _ _ _ _ _ _ _

PSERSXE   _ _ _ _ _ _ _

YISMEL   _ _ _ _ _ _

YVILDEER   _ _ _ _ _ _ _ _

DNTRECDUIE   _ _ _ _ _ _ _ _ _ _

RRLUA   _ _ _ _ _

SREREV   _ _ _ _ _ _

EMDAIL   _ _ _ _ _ _

Puzzle #54
KIDS

UEIDOTLESER   _ _ _ _ _ _ _ _ _ _ _

SLUNEPFLASY   _ _ _ _ _ _ _ _ _ _ _

UCKLC   _ _ _ _ _

AHSDDIF   _ _ _ _ _ _ _

IMUROMEP   _ _ _ _ _ _ _ _

USNA   _ _ _ _

LEIABIRLL   _ _ _ _ _ _ _ _ _

PCHREAY   _ _ _ _ _ _ _

TSMAOC   _ _ _ _ _ _

PSTIL   _ _ _ _ _

ISRMSE   _ _ _ _ _ _

FFENEEVCIIT   _ _ _ _ _ _ _ _ _ _ _

UFDRRE   _ _ _ _ _ _

ASGP   _ _ _ _

NJUAOKIK   _ _ _ _ _ _ _ _

AKWCLAT   _ _ _ _ _ _ _

EETPRRSEN   _ _ _ _ _ _ _ _ _

AOREPLD   _ _ _ _ _ _ _

YTTKI   _ _ _ _ _

NBYO   _ _ _ _

IOCL   _ _ _ _

ITEAEYNSLSL   _ _ _ _ _ _ _ _ _ _ _

SCELKPE   _ _ _ _ _ _ _

PIWH   _ _ _ _

Puzzle #56
ISLAND HOPPING

ALMKOIO   _ _ _ _ _ _ _

OYLCASP   _ _ _ _ _ _ _

EFLNTOO   _ _ _ _ _ _ _

IAGNTUA   _ _ _ _ _ _ _

WRARON   _ _ _ _ _ _

CNLDAIE   _ _ _ _ _ _ _

IANRIITDADN   _ _ _ _ _ _ _ _ _ _ _

LEETYMIN   _ _ _ _ _ _ _ _

SUHOT   _ _ _ _ _

TNAAHIIT   _ _ _ _ _ _ _ _

SHOP   _ _ _ _

CDOIAINM   _ _ _ _ _ _ _ _

CALENDAR

ATUMHZM   _ _ _ _ _ _ _

KPYSEFLC   _ _ _ _ _ _ _ _

ECKOTD   _ _ _ _ _ _

RAIEMIFR   _ _ _ _ _ _ _ _

TEASVH   _ _ _ _ _ _

RIARAANG   _ _ _ _ _ _ _ _

MOERSSID   _ _ _ _ _ _ _ _

MARSK   _ _ _ _ _

UARJANY   _ _ _ _ _ _ _

XIEDF   _ _ _ _ _

FIARE   _ _ _ _ _

AUILNJ   _ _ _ _ _ _

Puzzle #58
GREAT MOMENT

OHRU   _ _ _ _

KCUD   _ _ _ _

ERIW   _ _ _ _

TAYEHR   _ _ _ _ _ _

TELIJBUA   _ _ _ _ _ _ _ _

EIWS   _ _ _ _

EOHEBNKARRT   _ _ _ _ _ _ _ _ _ _ _

PODE   _ _ _ _

ABTSL   _ _ _ _ _

OLNEUCSV   _ _ _ _ _ _ _ _

GEMIUNDTA   _ _ _ _ _ _ _ _ _

GNOMCI   _ _ _ _ _ _

CARTOON

TENSUEISTON

_ _ _ _ _ _ _ _ _ _ _

ADNINISYCTO

_ _ _ _ _ _ _ _ _ _ _

VNALI

_ _ _ _ _

IATMRNOA

_ _ _ _ _ _ _ _

IBMPL

_ _ _ _ _

EYNCSITAD

_ _ _ _ _ _ _ _ _

IDEOAITN

_ _ _ _ _ _ _ _

YREMANDGERR

_ _ _ _ _ _ _ _ _ _ _

POITMEE

_ _ _ _ _ _ _

WOMANEPR

_ _ _ _ _ _ _ _

DESPSEI

_ _ _ _ _ _ _

VSILUA

_ _ _ _ _ _

Puzzle #60
AGRICULTURE

RRIAAGNA   _ _ _ _ _ _ _ _

INTGILS   _ _ _ _ _ _ _

OPAHTS   _ _ _ _ _ _

HARNYBDSU   _ _ _ _ _ _ _ _ _

TRSAO   _ _ _ _ _

REKAB   _ _ _ _ _

OMANID   _ _ _ _ _ _

RUCUTEL   _ _ _ _ _ _ _

UINESLTBAAS   _ _ _ _ _ _ _ _ _ _ _

TSKOC   _ _ _ _ _

BOOT   _ _ _ _

GABOOLYORIG   _ _ _ _ _ _ _ _ _ _ _

AHCROCNE   _ _ _ _ _ _ _ _

KRMA   _ _ _ _

SEKRIT   _ _ _ _ _ _

TSIGRA   _ _ _ _ _ _

ATNTDE   _ _ _ _ _ _

KRSMEO   _ _ _ _ _ _

ITGTENS   _ _ _ _ _ _ _

QIEUR   _ _ _ _ _

NRLVEAIT   _ _ _ _ _ _ _ _

ORSONTC   _ _ _ _ _ _ _

UAUIMTODRI   _ _ _ _ _ _ _ _ _ _

EVERDERS   _ _ _ _ _ _ _ _

Puzzle #62
OUTDOOR GEAR ACTIVIT

LPAARPE   _ _ _ _ _ _ _

OGORUB   _ _ _ _ _ _

ARNEA   _ _ _ _ _

DAANYRL   _ _ _ _ _ _ _

EILANTR   _ _ _ _ _ _ _

BEFOIRN   _ _ _ _ _ _ _

EWAAYRA   _ _ _ _ _ _ _

SOATR   _ _ _ _ _

CIRPPLE   _ _ _ _ _ _ _

CLNAE   _ _ _ _ _

RDYA   _ _ _ _

LCIREHHATSG   _ _ _ _ _ _ _ _ _ _ _

Puzzle #63
SALAD

MNAEIDEOC   _ _ _ _ _ _ _ _ _

EVIDEN   _ _ _ _ _ _

PIOPRAR   _ _ _ _ _ _ _

RALUUGA   _ _ _ _ _ _ _

CETUBTONIR   _ _ _ _ _ _ _ _ _ _

PFIINERTG   _ _ _ _ _ _ _ _ _

EATANUECCT   _ _ _ _ _ _ _ _ _ _

EHAGCR   _ _ _ _ _ _

BCUMCUER   _ _ _ _ _ _ _ _

EULCTTE   _ _ _ _ _ _ _

OUKILVAS   _ _ _ _ _ _ _ _

ALZCO   _ _ _ _ _

Puzzle #64
COMPUTER

ROERRAMGMP   _ _ _ _ _ _ _ _ _ _

OECXNEUTI   _ _ _ _ _ _ _ _ _

XEIT   _ _ _ _

MYRIRBCEEC   _ _ _ _ _ _ _ _ _ _

CIAHRPG   _ _ _ _ _ _ _

MEAULTE   _ _ _ _ _ _ _

TEATSCSE   _ _ _ _ _ _ _ _

VNSOII   _ _ _ _ _ _

NADHHEDL   _ _ _ _ _ _ _ _

OITMIZPE   _ _ _ _ _ _ _ _

SUERBTR   _ _ _ _ _ _ _

ENENGI   _ _ _ _ _ _

SUPER CAR

SHNCROCIG   _ _ _ _ _ _ _ _ _

TLSABAL   _ _ _ _ _ _ _

SLWO   _ _ _ _

YAEDESWP   _ _ _ _ _ _ _ _

ELSORS   _ _ _ _ _ _

FORO   _ _ _ _

IRGP   _ _ _ _

RNTE   _ _ _ _

AOCRNH   _ _ _ _ _ _

BXCAOR   _ _ _ _ _ _

LDDOEA   _ _ _ _ _ _

ARCSH   _ _ _ _ _

Puzzle #66
ANIMAL

TTDECAUSRAN   _ _ _ _ _ _ _ _ _ _ _

EIRHSF   _ _ _ _ _ _

RONRCAI   _ _ _ _ _ _ _

TOAC   _ _ _ _

TLNVEA   _ _ _ _ _ _

EBTI   _ _ _ _

NALTO   _ _ _ _ _ _

EAGRES   _ _ _ _ _ _

ANHHUC   _ _ _ _ _ _

LLTAS   _ _ _ _ _

MMYMU   _ _ _ _ _

RARIUAVESN   _ _ _ _ _ _ _ _ _ _

Puzzle #67
COOKING

OMSIEANL   _ _ _ _ _ _ _ _

EVLID   _ _ _ _ _

EMOGTRU   _ _ _ _ _ _ _

HRECNF   _ _ _ _ _ _

LSAE   _ _ _ _

OEDUNF   _ _ _ _ _ _

DODNES   _ _ _ _ _ _

OADMNL   _ _ _ _ _ _

VOCRKEOO   _ _ _ _ _ _ _ _

ETLCRAE   _ _ _ _ _ _ _

TESW   _ _ _ _

BROGEA   _ _ _ _ _ _

Puzzle #68
MOON

MSTLEETTEN   _ _ _ _ _ _ _ _ _ _

PALTRAI   _ _ _ _ _ _ _

SPHAE   _ _ _ _ _

OTOR   _ _ _ _

MESIUCNS   _ _ _ _ _ _ _ _

AAVL   _ _ _ _

SICAODAUU   _ _ _ _ _ _ _ _ _

OCME   _ _ _ _

ENAW   _ _ _ _

AREGURL   _ _ _ _ _ _ _

HYESNGU   _ _ _ _ _ _ _

ELOMSNSO   _ _ _ _ _ _ _ _

Puzzle #69
HOME EXCHANGE

BSTPKCAO   _ _ _ _ _ _ _ _

EHSTE   _ _ _ _ _

OMLBEI   _ _ _ _ _ _

AHTHRE   _ _ _ _ _ _

MHEO   _ _ _ _

ELIXE   _ _ _ _ _

ELIRECTD   _ _ _ _ _ _ _ _

RDINLEE   _ _ _ _ _ _ _

BBRIE   _ _ _ _ _

NRCYUREC   _ _ _ _ _ _ _ _

UOMNMEC   _ _ _ _ _ _ _

SDAGAR   _ _ _ _ _ _

Puzzle #70
NAVY

MAARDA   _ _ _ _ _ _

CESREPN   _ _ _ _ _ _ _

LLLFAOIT   _ _ _ _ _ _ _ _

AIANRM   _ _ _ _ _ _

ENAMRI   _ _ _ _ _ _

AIORVTA   _ _ _ _ _ _ _

SSIREPM   _ _ _ _ _ _ _

JIMYM   _ _ _ _ _

SALE   _ _ _ _

FRELANEU   _ _ _ _ _ _ _ _

ALORGOYE   _ _ _ _ _ _ _ _

MHINICTAS   _ _ _ _ _ _ _ _ _

CLASSROOM

MISOTRDOFC

_ _ _ _ _ _ _ _ _ _

HRTIALYI

_ _ _ _ _ _ _ _

CLOMHOORSO

_ _ _ _ _ _ _ _ _ _

NGAMEMITS

_ _ _ _ _ _ _ _ _

EFRKWLIOD

_ _ _ _ _ _ _ _ _

ODLDTE

_ _ _ _ _ _

COLKC

_ _ _ _ _

UOCSAUR

_ _ _ _ _ _ _

CTROEJP

_ _ _ _ _ _ _

CCOIMSIRCMO

_ _ _ _ _ _ _ _ _ _ _

OPRPVEA

_ _ _ _ _ _ _

IATMANNI

_ _ _ _ _ _ _ _

SAMOCPS _ _ _ _ _ _ _

ODOW _ _ _ _

IYRLTCEEF _ _ _ _ _ _ _ _ _

IEPERSR _ _ _ _ _ _ _

INUAICMS _ _ _ _ _ _ _ _

TNIPO _ _ _ _ _

PPINIG _ _ _ _ _ _

AGRYLN _ _ _ _ _ _

RMSUT _ _ _ _ _

DEAPL _ _ _ _ _

UFIALRG _ _ _ _ _ _ _

NARSEHP _ _ _ _ _ _ _

Puzzle #73
LEARN ENGLISH

ITRCETO   _ _ _ _ _ _ _

NRAIKLNF   _ _ _ _ _ _ _ _

CCHAE   _ _ _ _ _

GEEREN   _ _ _ _ _ _

EIEPNXCREE   _ _ _ _ _ _ _ _ _ _

EOLD   _ _ _ _

SIWE   _ _ _ _

UTPKEA   _ _ _ _ _ _

ORLYAT   _ _ _ _ _ _

NPOSO   _ _ _ _ _

CTERRA   _ _ _ _ _ _

DOHAWR   _ _ _ _ _ _

Puzzle #74
SIMPLE LIVING

EPODRAYTR   _ _ _ _ _ _ _ _ _

EFRHCN   _ _ _ _ _ _

NENEIDPNTED   _ _ _ _ _ _ _ _ _ _ _

MRANEG   _ _ _ _ _ _

HISTMAIN   _ _ _ _ _ _ _ _

EANPTR   _ _ _ _ _ _

PLAIEART   _ _ _ _ _ _ _ _

DDPREETA   _ _ _ _ _ _ _ _

MRIT   _ _ _ _

ADBN   _ _ _ _

OERV   _ _ _ _

CCANILLI   _ _ _ _ _ _ _ _

INTERIOR DESIGN

SEEERVSLNC   _ _ _ _ _ _ _ _ _ _

TROP   _ _ _ _

MHATC   _ _ _ _ _

UOFEORSCOPL   _ _ _ _ _ _ _ _ _ _ _

RYFOEWL   _ _ _ _ _ _ _

EMRIMRT   _ _ _ _ _ _ _

AYMZ   _ _ _ _

NULPDA   _ _ _ _ _ _

YEPT   _ _ _ _

ODURWSAT   _ _ _ _ _ _ _ _

GTLIANOI   _ _ _ _ _ _ _ _

WOCAOTLRER   _ _ _ _ _ _ _ _ _ _

Puzzle #76
HOLIDAY

UOCLM   _ _ _ _ _

NEAEINVLT   _ _ _ _ _ _ _ _ _

ZOMTA   _ _ _ _ _

TSRROE   _ _ _ _ _ _

SEPEKKEA   _ _ _ _ _ _ _ _

DUEBSU   _ _ _ _ _ _

RECEOC   _ _ _ _ _ _

VREEERNEG   _ _ _ _ _ _ _ _ _

TAEK   _ _ _ _

KWAE   _ _ _ _

EIRAVIR   _ _ _ _ _ _ _

OEVSBRE   _ _ _ _ _ _ _

Puzzle #77
MOTOCYCLE RACING

NLIENGEUY   _ _ _ _ _ _ _ _ _

HYIDNG   _ _ _ _ _ _

NIGTRA   _ _ _ _ _ _

TOUBOKDS   _ _ _ _ _ _ _ _

HAKC   _ _ _ _

NOREBK   _ _ _ _ _ _

RSESP   _ _ _ _ _

BMROKKAEO   _ _ _ _ _ _ _ _ _

CRSUTNTCORO   _ _ _ _ _ _ _ _ _ _ _

KLSI   _ _ _ _

EEHLVCI   _ _ _ _ _ _ _

OKOIEB   _ _ _ _ _ _

Puzzle #78
ENVIRONMENT POLLUTIO

NISAOOACITS   _ _ _ _ _ _ _ _ _ _ _

PITACVYIT   _ _ _ _ _ _ _ _ _

FDLEI   _ _ _ _ _

EITDEEMFLN   _ _ _ _ _ _ _ _ _ _

UNCEALP   _ _ _ _ _ _ _

IOSENRTRIAP   _ _ _ _ _ _ _ _ _ _ _

UNROUSRD   _ _ _ _ _ _ _ _

TOIALGENNC   _ _ _ _ _ _ _ _ _ _

ICEMANEB   _ _ _ _ _ _ _ _

ALITHYLCE   _ _ _ _ _ _ _ _ _

LRUAMISTO   _ _ _ _ _ _ _ _ _

TLESEIR   _ _ _ _ _ _ _

BEAUTY

CBNEIAT

_ _ _ _ _ _ _

SIGN

_ _ _ _

ENGAETL

_ _ _ _ _ _ _

EIDSDPNL

_ _ _ _ _ _ _ _

MOCICTSE

_ _ _ _ _ _ _ _

OLMARGU

_ _ _ _ _ _ _

FLEE

_ _ _ _

SPERO

_ _ _ _ _

PGTEAAN

_ _ _ _ _ _ _

ROLGY

_ _ _ _ _

TNCTENTASO

_ _ _ _ _ _ _ _ _ _

ADUOTWR

_ _ _ _ _ _ _

Puzzle #80
MAGIC TRICKS

MASH   _ _ _ _

RUCCIS   _ _ _ _ _ _

CTUCLO   _ _ _ _ _ _

NHEOTIIIXB   _ _ _ _ _ _ _ _ _ _

IANRT   _ _ _ _ _

LGNAEW   _ _ _ _ _ _

ONMEG   _ _ _ _ _

IOSBILMAD   _ _ _ _ _ _ _ _ _

JOSNHNO   _ _ _ _ _ _ _

TSAMIO   _ _ _ _ _ _

TRFCA   _ _ _ _ _

DDEGO   _ _ _ _ _

Puzzle #81
BALLOON

DHEATEHIGDL   _ _ _ _ _ _ _ _ _ _ _

RBSTU   _ _ _ _ _

GAASNBD   _ _ _ _ _ _ _

IGTILPNFU   _ _ _ _ _ _ _ _ _

IENFRTS   _ _ _ _ _ _ _

UCSAFRE   _ _ _ _ _ _ _

LTFI   _ _ _ _

DNTMIENYI   _ _ _ _ _ _ _ _ _

IURTDG   _ _ _ _ _ _

KALE   _ _ _ _

LOKYLJI   _ _ _ _ _ _ _

LENIATF   _ _ _ _ _ _ _

CHINA

NTIAINJ

_ _ _ _ _ _ _

AAKRAOKMR

_ _ _ _ _ _ _ _ _

KIATN

_ _ _ _ _

NGNGTKWUA

_ _ _ _ _ _ _ _ _

IAHJKISRNI

_ _ _ _ _ _ _ _ _ _

NNUAH

_ _ _ _ _

NCMAUH

_ _ _ _ _ _

TMJUCAN

_ _ _ _ _ _ _

IWWLAEWLOR

_ _ _ _ _ _ _ _ _ _

LUANIR

_ _ _ _ _ _

ICER

_ _ _ _

GNUS

_ _ _ _

NMNWOI   _ _ _ _ _ _

SALPOLC   _ _ _ _ _ _ _

DIOPNCIYR   _ _ _ _ _ _ _ _ _

EIHFLIKS   _ _ _ _ _ _ _ _

FDSPNIHO   _ _ _ _ _ _ _ _

CKOO   _ _ _ _

ALSCE   _ _ _ _ _

FIPSHAERS   _ _ _ _ _ _ _ _ _

SLAHO   _ _ _ _ _

HFOSRBAI   _ _ _ _ _ _ _ _

WFAELIE   _ _ _ _ _ _ _

CCDYOLI   _ _ _ _ _ _ _

MOUNTAIN

DGIEU　　　　　　　_ _ _ _ _

GORIBNH　　　　　_ _ _ _ _ _ _

HRAKCATD　　　　_ _ _ _ _ _ _ _

BVINLISIE　　　　_ _ _ _ _ _ _ _ _

TEBUT　　　　　　_ _ _ _ _

SMJAAA　　　　　_ _ _ _ _ _

ACCSAUUS　　　　_ _ _ _ _ _ _ _

NTLENU　　　　　_ _ _ _ _ _

ATOMRNTANE　　　_ _ _ _ _ _ _ _ _ _

TLWRESHI　　　　_ _ _ _ _ _ _ _

KAERB　　　　　　_ _ _ _ _

MUOTASEN　　　　_ _ _ _ _ _ _ _

FASHION

OIUNDCGRFE _ _ _ _ _ _ _ _ _ _

ELFRTTU _ _ _ _ _ _ _

AQNBUET _ _ _ _ _ _ _

TDIAM _ _ _ _ _

LKOO _ _ _ _

ARBW _ _ _ _

CIOCEIND _ _ _ _ _ _ _ _

SURPEDLMEO _ _ _ _ _ _ _ _ _ _

AERNTTP _ _ _ _ _ _ _

GDFELNEWAN _ _ _ _ _ _ _ _ _ _

YNURAW _ _ _ _ _ _

EDAUNTD _ _ _ _ _ _ _

Puzzle #86
BATHROOM

YPOTT   _ _ _ _ _

WSBSAAHIN   _ _ _ _ _ _ _ _ _

MATPENRTA   _ _ _ _ _ _ _ _ _

AYRBNI   _ _ _ _ _ _

NISK   _ _ _ _

STHEITR   _ _ _ _ _ _ _

VTSOE   _ _ _ _ _

ELRZVEBAI   _ _ _ _ _ _ _ _ _

EEDENNDNTIP   _ _ _ _ _ _ _ _ _ _ _

EVRIPETEIT   _ _ _ _ _ _ _ _ _ _

NPUGREL   _ _ _ _ _ _ _

OLIZEBMMII   _ _ _ _ _ _ _ _ _ _

Puzzle #87
TRAVEL

IROBT   _ _ _ _ _

CCHTA   _ _ _ _ _

EPLACUS   _ _ _ _ _ _ _

RIESVCE   _ _ _ _ _ _ _

BOBM   _ _ _ _

OSAENS   _ _ _ _ _ _

AIPRRE   _ _ _ _ _ _

KRSEIT   _ _ _ _ _ _

TIPR   _ _ _ _

URCEIRO   _ _ _ _ _ _ _

TRENREY   _ _ _ _ _ _ _

ORTLOAC   _ _ _ _ _ _ _

Puzzle #88
TELEVISION

RSESIE   _ _ _ _ _ _

LREASI   _ _ _ _ _ _

IKLN   _ _ _ _

IUSALV   _ _ _ _ _ _

LYAIDSP   _ _ _ _ _ _ _

CEMCRDOAR   _ _ _ _ _ _ _ _ _

FONRT   _ _ _ _ _

TPRERROE   _ _ _ _ _ _ _ _

NOOWRSME   _ _ _ _ _ _ _ _

NECEPRITO   _ _ _ _ _ _ _ _ _

NIATRG   _ _ _ _ _ _

MOURF   _ _ _ _ _

ELECTRIC BIKES

EMSGRNEES   _ _ _ _ _ _ _ _ _

LTVO   _ _ _ _

HENEDUGRACR   _ _ _ _ _ _ _ _ _ _ _

BXEOIC   _ _ _ _ _ _

MSBEASLE   _ _ _ _ _ _ _ _

ECHOATD   _ _ _ _ _ _ _

FREAIMN   _ _ _ _ _ _ _

OALRP   _ _ _ _ _

EILCALRCTE   _ _ _ _ _ _ _ _ _ _

HGAERDC   _ _ _ _ _ _ _

NIFEFDERINT   _ _ _ _ _ _ _ _ _ _ _

EPMGRAAE   _ _ _ _ _ _ _ _

ANTI AGING

UKNP

_ _ _ _

EDRUS

_ _ _ _ _

REEGSSR

_ _ _ _ _ _ _

RZTEFAINEE

_ _ _ _ _ _ _ _ _ _

SETOCORNI

_ _ _ _ _ _ _ _ _

BTIAICIONT

_ _ _ _ _ _ _ _ _ _

ALLTIFP

_ _ _ _ _ _ _

MOSTOH

_ _ _ _ _ _

TSITRIHRA

_ _ _ _ _ _ _ _ _

IANT

_ _ _ _

RGOEU

_ _ _ _ _

NFIOUERBP

_ _ _ _ _ _ _ _ _

Puzzle #91
ARTIFICIAL INTELLIGE

TEAT   _ _ _ _

ATMOUN   _ _ _ _ _ _

XPACEIOTNLE   _ _ _ _ _ _ _ _ _ _ _

CYEWARA   _ _ _ _ _ _ _

CDDOBRAAR   _ _ _ _ _ _ _ _ _

VERSESCNLE   _ _ _ _ _ _ _ _ _ _

KNIGONW   _ _ _ _ _ _ _

LTISSWE   _ _ _ _ _ _ _

IALYWCUES   _ _ _ _ _ _ _ _ _

OCUKOC   _ _ _ _ _ _

NIOISV   _ _ _ _ _ _

NTHAMTDEOU   _ _ _ _ _ _ _ _ _ _

Puzzle #92
TRUCK

NERATK   _ _ _ _ _ _

EDISLE   _ _ _ _ _ _

LDOMA   _ _ _ _ _

AGLONDO   _ _ _ _ _ _ _

LIEN   _ _ _ _

RKRCTUE   _ _ _ _ _ _ _

ITHMENSP   _ _ _ _ _ _ _ _

SMPDRETU   _ _ _ _ _ _ _ _

ETARRB   _ _ _ _ _ _

PCOH   _ _ _ _

ECKER   _ _ _ _ _

HARTWDROOY   _ _ _ _ _ _ _ _ _ _

OFFICE

CAPOIITTFEN

_ _ _ _ _ _ _ _ _ _

RHNYAROO

_ _ _ _ _ _ _ _

PDAOT

_ _ _ _ _

SPDHHIEA

_ _ _ _ _ _ _ _

CSRJYITIAU

_ _ _ _ _ _ _ _ _ _

SAWRDNPEIH

_ _ _ _ _ _ _ _ _ _

ITNVSE

_ _ _ _ _ _

HBNEC

_ _ _ _ _

NAUHTEGSO

_ _ _ _ _ _ _ _ _

DSOMIITAPLT

_ _ _ _ _ _ _ _ _ _ _

PPAIANECL

_ _ _ _ _ _ _ _ _

ASCK

_ _ _ _

WORKING

ELVEA _ _ _ _ _

OAITNREPVEI _ _ _ _ _ _ _ _ _ _

NSITAR _ _ _ _ _ _

GABREE _ _ _ _ _ _

CETSRE _ _ _ _ _ _

RANK _ _ _ _

ESOTIMUCUL _ _ _ _ _ _ _ _ _ _

ITONTDAE _ _ _ _ _ _ _ _

FASNAREGI _ _ _ _ _ _ _ _ _

EROC _ _ _ _

WKRREO _ _ _ _ _ _

NBIDBO _ _ _ _ _ _

PIEPYU

_ _ _ _ _ _

RTNOFUE

_ _ _ _ _ _ _

AGLGINFG

_ _ _ _ _ _ _ _

CAME

_ _ _ _

RALET

_ _ _ _ _

RESVDIA

_ _ _ _ _ _ _

REITER

_ _ _ _ _ _

ULAIIDCJR

_ _ _ _ _ _ _ _ _

RNYJUI

_ _ _ _ _ _

EMETNTEIRR

_ _ _ _ _ _ _ _ _ _

ICATVOON

_ _ _ _ _ _ _ _

OHEW

_ _ _ _

Puzzle #96
COWBOY HATS

CPLAAA   _ _ _ _ _ _

VAEWE   _ _ _ _ _

XBDBANO   _ _ _ _ _ _ _

RIETTAEG   _ _ _ _ _ _ _ _

RDWLA   _ _ _ _ _

ANOLLOB   _ _ _ _ _ _ _

KINT   _ _ _ _

RLTNCCAEUE   _ _ _ _ _ _ _ _ _ _

NHAFOMF   _ _ _ _ _ _ _

CKOLB   _ _ _ _ _

OLBGEI   _ _ _ _ _ _

SDAAHLLTN   _ _ _ _ _ _ _ _ _

Puzzle #97
ESTATE PLANNING

EHITNEQCU   _ _ _ _ _ _ _ _ _

AENAWOLLC   _ _ _ _ _ _ _ _ _

ONJIERUT   _ _ _ _ _ _ _ _

ECSLO   _ _ _ _ _

ICSNYD   _ _ _ _ _ _

ITTRENSE   _ _ _ _ _ _ _ _

BORNYA   _ _ _ _ _ _

INDAOM   _ _ _ _ _ _

HOISOGNT   _ _ _ _ _ _ _ _

TRHIREO   _ _ _ _ _ _ _

TERTEEMBTN   _ _ _ _ _ _ _ _ _ _

GINIXF   _ _ _ _ _ _

Puzzle #98
FILM MAKING

UYDTSR   _ _ _ _ _ _

LERLOR   _ _ _ _ _ _

CUARNFUTEAM   _ _ _ _ _ _ _ _ _ _

DIGANWD   _ _ _ _ _ _ _

LNSUMAOJRI   _ _ _ _ _ _ _ _ _

AEGMI   _ _ _ _ _

ISNCNSNALEO   _ _ _ _ _ _ _ _ _ _

SENVRTATII   _ _ _ _ _ _ _ _ _

ORLIPFAEBT   _ _ _ _ _ _ _ _ _ _

LPIB   _ _ _ _

RAKTC   _ _ _ _ _

TIDADICC   _ _ _ _ _ _ _ _

Puzzle #99
CASUAL DINING

NNOFROTEA   _ _ _ _ _ _ _ _ _

ASREPIT   _ _ _ _ _ _ _

UNSH   _ _ _ _

NTCTNEGOIN   _ _ _ _ _ _ _ _ _ _

ATRRNUSATE   _ _ _ _ _ _ _ _ _ _

PILF   _ _ _ _

ANMDOR   _ _ _ _ _ _

YAROTAHWW   _ _ _ _ _ _ _ _ _

OSNG   _ _ _ _

HTEOPCPRI   _ _ _ _ _ _ _ _ _

RTSPO   _ _ _ _ _

REITSK   _ _ _ _ _ _

HOSPITAL

IAILPEZHTOS _ _ _ _ _ _ _ _ _ _

SYROANAITT _ _ _ _ _ _ _ _ _ _

UEATRNAQIN _ _ _ _ _ _ _ _ _ _

ITSIACPTNE _ _ _ _ _ _ _ _ _ _

EMTAIN _ _ _ _ _ _

IGENDDB _ _ _ _ _ _ _

RATRES _ _ _ _ _ _

RXENTE _ _ _ _ _ _

IREECVGRA _ _ _ _ _ _ _ _ _

OIOSVARBNTE _ _ _ _ _ _ _ _ _ _ _

AEATRLNM _ _ _ _ _ _ _ _

ERCA _ _ _ _

Puzzle # 1
WRESTLING

BTUO	=	BOUT
ROEP	=	ROPE
STHTIEAN	=	HESITANT
PTOS	=	STOP
SLCFFUE	=	SCUFFLE
RYAADRVSE	=	ADVERSARY
CHIP	=	CHIP
AESV	=	SAVE
EVALT	=	VALET
ERLSTEEYF	=	FREESTYLE
NGRI	=	RING
DNWO	=	DOWN

WINSUMOPJGH	=	SHOWJUMPING
RUJPME	=	JUMPER
NEICDLU	=	INCLUDE
NRNOTAPSOS	=	TRANSPOSON
RARMONSTB	=	BARNSTORM
KYNAGHAM	=	GYMKHANA
EARH	=	HARE
SLOUE	=	LOUSE
PUNEOC	=	POUNCE
RPAROPATERO	=	PARATROOPER
HLMAA	=	HALMA
AFLE	=	FLEA

AEGER	=	AGREE
RAAROTIDIIN	=	IRRADIATION
SRIAYOVNI	=	VISIONARY
ERRIMP	=	PRIMER
ASREENGT	=	ESTRANGE
ISPEIDLC	=	DISCIPLE
KCOLB	=	BLOCK
HCCITEANNI	=	TECHNICIAN
STPLIO	=	SPOILT
GEDBDAIR	=	ABRIDGED
UITBNLI	=	INBUILT
FITDR	=	DRIFT

Puzzle # 4
SAVING MONEY

BCUL = CLUB

ONUTIBFUL = BOUNTIFUL

SIGINNK = SINKING

SREKTI = STRIKE

LBWO = BLOW

TWIEH = WHITE

DPRO = DROP

LSTA = LATS

ZRSGO = GROSZ

OPAMRSYNI = PARSIMONY

DORINE = DINERO

DMRA = DRAM

Puzzle # 5
CALIFORNIA

NAAP	=	NAPA
HACIBSL	=	CHABLIS
AHDTAFE	=	FATHEAD
CTJSKELAM	=	JACKSMELT
IADCLHPR	=	PILCHARD
ONARAMPIS	=	MARIPOSAN
CFAIL	=	CALIF
OWOBOIBDNR	=	RIBBONWOOD
WASTT	=	WATTS
APUH	=	HUPA
WIOKM	=	MIWOK
MYAO	=	MAYO

Puzzle # 6
SELF DEFENSE

TABAGRRG	=	BRAGGART
HOANGTEP	=	HEPTAGON
NLTAFULTE	=	FLATULENT
RREVOCE	=	RECOVER
EYBO	=	OBEY
OFTR	=	FORT
UCRDPNTEOTE	=	UNPROTECTED
IRTADAZME	=	DRAMATIZE
ALRITIV	=	TRIVIAL
CNTOITNEN	=	CONTINENT
SUOISLAYT	=	AUTOLYSIS
NIVTOIDINCA	=	VINDICATION

Puzzle # 7
PRESSURE COOKER

SPIULXNEO	=	EXPULSION
ITLSRPEMSA	=	SLIPSTREAM
LGUBE	=	BULGE
CMPITANH	=	PITCHMAN
RESSURPE	=	PRESSURE
ZEGNEQSIU	=	SQUEEZING
RENDTIGA	=	GRADIENT
FCIDALC	=	FLACCID
ILOPT	=	PILOT
GYRINES	=	SYRINGE
SRATT	=	START
ORBTIAV	=	VIBRATO

OIALPDM	=	DIPLOMA
MALE	=	LAME
BURN	=	BURN
EALCD	=	DECAL
YTPTOER	=	POTTERY
INEFACE	=	FAIENCE
YACL	=	CLAY
TNLIF	=	FLINT
EFOSONT	=	FESTOON
RFUTAAEUMCN	=	MANUFACTURE
MYAA	=	MAYA
GEIARZL	=	GLAZIER

WIND SURFING

KCRAN	=	CRANK
OGOHTD	=	HOTDOG
IOBNBB	=	BOBBIN
AHLU	=	HAUL
UAECRITNOT	=	ERUCTATION
RAEG	=	RAGE
KKCI	=	KICK
ITDRF	=	DRIFT
TNEURSHO	=	SOUTHERN
PSRA	=	RASP
REOWCRSKC	=	CORKSCREW
GTUSY	=	GUSTY

Puzzle # 10
PACKING LIST

SCTRIP	=	SCRIPT
NOWD	=	DOWN
KANR	=	RANK
CNEFLIT	=	INFLECT
EMRONTELN	=	ENROLMENT
AEMLM	=	LEMMA
AMEPHR	=	HAMPER
ENLCBAA	=	BALANCE
EOUSHLERC	=	LECHEROUS
LISO	=	SILO
TCRNIECU	=	CINCTURE
EISMDED	=	MISDEED

UNPPETDA	=	UNTAPPED
BODDIE	=	BODIED
HTRGEAIEM	=	HERMITAGE
SEPEAIXNV	=	EXPANSIVE
RCOOEL	=	COOLER
ACRLY	=	CLARY
ELSE	=	LEES
TAPA	=	TAPA
GSEDAO	=	DOSAGE
AEARMDI	=	MADEIRA
ALSBLBYU	=	SYLLABUB
STNIA	=	STAIN

Puzzle # 12
BUILDING

KHOO	=	HOOK
REIP	=	PIER
EYVNIR	=	VINERY
TNGAIES	=	SEATING
HFSIUNR	=	FURNISH
RIROTEEX	=	EXTERIOR
ICANMAOHR	=	HARMONICA
REEOLDM	=	REMODEL
RAREFT	=	RAFTER
TAECSL	=	CASTLE
DHFEEOLERR	=	FREEHOLDER
ENRAANECYTW	=	ENTRANCEWAY

COLLEGE SCHOLARSHIPS

NDHNOIS	=	DONNISH
OTRUT	=	TUTOR
TSFAF	=	STAFF
MNMOOC	=	COMMON
UAEEDTC	=	EDUCATE
CYDAAEM	=	ACADEMY
PEELX	=	EXPEL
LGAUETOCA	=	CATALOGUE
ENDAWR	=	WARDEN
RUTRICE	=	RECRUIT
ATROHIRCLE	=	RHETORICAL
SHONUGI	=	HOUSING

Puzzle # 14
PIZZA

OYODNB   =   NOBODY

EIWLEKIS   =   LIKEWISE

IUQLDSA   =   SQUALID

ARAVLOPP   =   APPROVAL

OURCYT   =   OUTCRY

ICHN   =   INCH

TRPEEHA   =   PREHEAT

AMALORLEZZ   =   MOZZARELLA

RIVAELABIN   =   INVARIABLE

VIELO   =   OLIVE

REONCEUN   =   RENOUNCE

RIDWE   =   WEIRD

Puzzle # 15
SPECIAL OCCASIONS

HTORWEYNOT	=	NOTEWORTHY
UGNNICN	=	CUNNING
URIEMPM	=	PREMIUM
RALME	=	REALM
HSPIOTLGT	=	SPOTLIGHT
TIFTENCO	=	CONFETTI
PTOSTY	=	SPOTTY
VERVE	=	VERVE
ONPTI	=	POINT
SEUCRE	=	SECURE
DRBROAOATRM	=	MORTARBOARD
CSOHEN	=	CHOSEN

Puzzle # 16
MAPS

AETS   =   EAST

GSYMROCAHPO   =   COSMOGRAPHY

NPOTRIICDE   =   PREDICTION

HRAYD   =   HYDRA

ITITNYED   =   IDENTITY

SIKKO   =   KIOSK

RIHPGCAS   =   GRAPHICS

EELFRI   =   RELIEF

TSAAL   =   ATLAS

WAHEERT   =   WEATHER

LPBREUISH   =   PUBLISHER

CSMSPAO   =   COMPASS

Puzzle # 17
CLEANING SUPPLIES

TCESKRO	=	STOCKER
LTAARIEM	=	MATERIAL
URPSREEAKMT	=	SUPERMARKET
TUOBBMA	=	BUMBOAT
HAKNY	=	HANKY
RMAWER	=	WARMER
OBCM	=	COMB
ROAEFG	=	FORAGE
SEFL	=	SELF
LUIBT	=	BUILT
REOCRG	=	GROCER
ILANEGNSC	=	CLEANSING

LMIF   =   FILM

IKCHT   =   THICK

TNTTAIA   =   ATTAINT

ECVOR   =   COVER

MTTLEO   =   MOTTLE

MIMSAA   =   MIASMA

BIUSNM   =   NIMBUS

KMRU   =   MURK

AKNB   =   BANK

OVRE   =   OVER

NISSHENU   =   SUNSHINE

KDENRA   =   DARKEN

FUNNY

OPSFO	=	SPOOF
RAHC	=	ARCH
IMIBTELLAIL	=	ILLIMITABLE
FDTA	=	DAFT
TAYLS	=	SALTY
ETVRERINER	=	IRREVERENT
WTIYT	=	WITTY
NUGAYTH	=	NAUGHTY
NELVAE	=	LEAVEN
UOOFBFN	=	BUFFOON
HIAQNEURL	=	HARLEQUIN
BECAICR	=	ACERBIC

Puzzle # 20
SHIRT

ISEKRPP	=	SKIPPER
TKSCBLAIRH	=	BLACKSHIRT
RJASDTUE	=	READJUST
MFNRLOAI	=	INFORMAL
NATAFK	=	KAFTAN
LATI	=	TAIL
AMRONO	=	MAROON
VDECINEE	=	EVIDENCE
BGYAG	=	BAGGY
UERTXTE	=	TEXTURE
SAJPMYA	=	PYJAMAS
OTCNOT	=	COTTON

BOUNDARIES

RILYALI	=	ILLYRIA
EURENIVS	=	UNIVERSE
NAOSHUTDLI	=	OUTLANDISH
RARTATY	=	TARTARY
FSUOPSLUUER	=	SUPERFLUOUS
HDYOYHARRPG	=	HYDROGRAPHY
NCNNEIFDUO	=	UNCONFINED
NSEDSLOBU	=	BOUNDLESS
TSGEEMN	=	SEGMENT
TELDBMEAT	=	EMBATTLED
IUDSNNGO	=	SOUNDING
UNIZADENGOR	=	UNORGANIZED

EGTIBRKLZI = BLITZKRIEG

TAECNEO = ACETONE

MOLTEI = MOTILE

CHURN = CHURN

XIELLFE = FLEXILE

KOLEIBOMOB = BOOKMOBILE

GUETNO = TONGUE

OAMPARECGH = MACROPHAGE

TTRHNESG = STRENGTH

IGONRDEDD = DODDERING

RYLOTAUMAB = AMBULATORY

CENET = CTENE

Puzzle # 23
BUILDING A HOUSE

EPIEC	=	PIECE
AGRRBUL	=	BURGLAR
SACFUE	=	FAUCES
EBEUTOSLN	=	BLUESTONE
RTTERU	=	TURRET
OEVLRTEA	=	ELEVATOR
LFTO	=	LOFT
EAMRHTEGI	=	HERMITAGE
IOPCLY	=	POLICY
OLSENTKE	=	SKELETON
KCED	=	DECK
ITRBATOA	=	ABATTOIR

Puzzle # 24
WRITING POETRY

OEATVC	=	OCTAVE
MFLOASYU	=	FAMOUSLY
ETCTRE	=	TERCET
HCGIPAR	=	GRAPHIC
TRASH	=	TRASH
KTSI	=	SKIT
MUVOOLSNIU	=	VOLUMINOUS
YERL	=	LYRE
AOTRNE	=	ORNATE
LBUL	=	BULL
IRPERM	=	PRIMER
ENTGUO	=	TONGUE

Puzzle # 25
PREGNANCY

TIAECNDC	=	ACCIDENT
TNNEOIEMNCF	=	CONFINEMENT
CNENOITCOP	=	CONCEPTION
NMLTRUAAIR	=	INTRAMURAL
CPERDSMEII	=	SPERMICIDE
EOYYGOLCGN	=	GYNECOLOGY
HMPAIRDAG	=	DIAPHRAGM
OLRAB	=	LABOR
NEMAALTR	=	MATERNAL
QAUD	=	QUAD
EIYHPERMSES	=	HYPEREMESIS
TYOOCFEPS	=	FETOSCOPY

KINGWNO	=	KNOWING
ANWF	=	FAWN
NERAY	=	YEARN
GFAL	=	FLAG
ECIPRH	=	CIPHER
LAAAITSN	=	ALSATIAN
RYROW	=	WORRY
RETROR	=	TERROR
ALENHDR	=	HANDLER
AOUNIUTLL	=	ULULATION
TBELKNA	=	BLANKET
CTEHF	=	FETCH

STPMIAB	=	BAPTISM
MMLSIU	=	MUSLIM
OTNOIVED	=	DEVOTION
IROPZYSLEET	=	PROSELYTIZE
FSLNIU	=	SINFUL
AANTHP	=	PATHAN
GIRLORNEII	=	IRRELIGION
ASEPL	=	LAPSE
IWENGKNAA	=	AWAKENING
HRMONAE	=	MENORAH
EESHYR	=	HERESY
SATCONIM	=	MONASTIC

LAWK	=	WALK
WAFRD	=	DWARF
IGTFED	=	GIFTED
IMCCO	=	COMIC
TDLUA	=	ADULT
ETRIFT	=	FITTER
AMEBYOONG	=	BOOGEYMAN
FNSEULF	=	SNUFFLE
LCALGRIE	=	ALLERGIC
BUBBYL	=	BUBBLY
EDPLIIAOPH	=	PEDOPHILIA
OTTIPE	=	TIPTOE

Puzzle # 29
BLOOD PRESSURE

ERHI	=	HEIR
ARZIIAHBL	=	BILHARZIA
THOCRE	=	HECTOR
HTBMOIRSSO	=	THROMBOSIS
OOLNES	=	LOOSEN
SSTSIPAYHO	=	HYPOSTASIS
SMAHS	=	SMASH
IURBME	=	IMBRUE
RNHEAD	=	HARDEN
UVCAEEAT	=	EVACUATE
ODLBYREBOR	=	BLOODBERRY
ITODVOLARAS	=	VASODILATOR

TLAUIQDEI	=	LIQUIDATE
TENER	=	RENTE
UTATSCIIOF	=	FACTITIOUS
CTEEEHPREN	=	THREEPENCE
TISKNLNFI	=	SKINFLINT
SPAMT	=	STAMP
CSELO	=	CLOSE
EEDERM	=	REDEEM
OTORM	=	MOTOR
OOBM	=	BOOM
ENVRTRDAUE	=	ADVENTURER
ALRI	=	RAIL

Puzzle # 31
ROMANTIC IDEAS

EPSPOO   =   OPPOSE

ACIATTNFS   =   FANTASTIC

LAIISETD   =   IDEALIST

ESEPSRX   =   EXPRESS

LSCDEO   =   CLOSED

LUSUOIMN   =   LUMINOUS

FIHGLTY   =   FLIGHTY

ELSLNWPIRG   =   WELLSPRING

AEDYMR   =   DREAMY

SMDIELIA   =   IDEALISM

EPSURIVO   =   PERVIOUS

LLCOAGI   =   LOGICAL

Puzzle # 32
TRAFFIC

TCAFOR	=	FACTOR
NDBIONU	=	INBOUND
OSTP	=	STOP
EDLIY	=	YIELD
AEMK	=	MAKE
DMOLEUAT	=	MODULATE
DOLEDTR	=	TODDLER
HIRSOOB	=	BOORISH
SYWPESXERA	=	EXPRESSWAY
AAMTTGSIRE	=	MAGISTRATE
LOTOFLAF	=	FOOTFALL
OITTNINTUIS	=	INSTITUTION

LYOG	=	LOGY
UPLL	=	PULL
RTSRAE	=	ARREST
TILO	=	TOIL
NTNAEDA	=	ANDANTE
AGFL	=	FLAG
KSELA	=	SLAKE
IRFITEBUSL	=	FILIBUSTER
ADHN	=	HAND
ADDWEL	=	DAWDLE
TAABE	=	ABATE
ALTSL	=	STALL

RBYED = DERBY

KEPIS = SPIKE

AEPESKR = SPEAKER

CLFFIAOI = OFFICIAL

XDFIE = FIXED

AKAYK = KAYAK

XBSKOY = SKYBOX

DWOASH = SHADOW

CORTNVE = CONVERT

ACKJ = JACK

EODM = DOME

PUPQIELA = APPLIQUE

MAGIC

RSSETSNEEAN	=	EARNESTNESS
ATAISMNL	=	TALISMAN
IENEG	=	GENIE
OEDRR	=	ORDER
ELATUIERRT	=	LITERATURE
UHIELM	=	HELIUM
CFOER	=	FORCE
VLEAITET	=	LEVITATE
RUCJNEO	=	CONJURE
CROJURNO	=	CONJUROR
TELAHLC	=	HELLCAT
ABDRACARAAB	=	ABRACADABRA

Puzzle # 36
PHOTOGRAPHY

RISETLB	=	BLISTER
BRCANGUDKO	=	BACKGROUND
UMHGOTS	=	MUGSHOT
RAODMKRO	=	DARKROOM
ONRMEMOCHO	=	MONOCHROME
CIATCIN	=	ACTINIC
ISIVNTESE	=	SENSITIVE
APOIGRRAHYD	=	RADIOGRAPHY
CEROETARLCA	=	ACCELERATOR
ESNSYZTIHE	=	SYNTHESIZE
INITTGS	=	SITTING
GTOAURRVERO	=	ROTOGRAVURE

MONEY

ADOTMEAOMCC	=	ACCOMMODATE
AEMBDRRESSA	=	EMBARRASSED
LODE	=	DOLE
RRIYE	=	EYRIR
BLUER	=	RUBLE
DIONEM	=	MONIED
CPLAE	=	PLACE
AENTRG	=	ARGENT
XDIFE	=	FIXED
IDASLA	=	DALASI
AHSL	=	LASH
EHINSR	=	SHINER

TRAIN

ARLTTRE = RATTLER

DORILARA = RAILROAD

AMOPRRG = PROGRAM

IGEUQPAE = EQUIPAGE

AKCB = BACK

EVER = VEER

LINEMSIOU = LIMOUSINE

ARTETCL = CLATTER

RUIEN = INURE

MCNETSEEAP = ESCAPEMENT

GDAREN = DANGER

SACEL = SCALE

Puzzle # 39
ARMY TRAINING

ITRTAITON	=	ATTRITION
ISAEGGNED	=	DISENGAGE
DDNHKCAE	=	DECKHAND
NRNAETUID	=	UNTRAINED
EMAEIHCZN	=	MECHANIZE
ODPDAKC	=	PADDOCK
EGABGAG	=	BAGGAGE
CHAOCIGN	=	COACHING
NCPSHIO	=	PHONICS
AJNAW	=	JAWAN
OTRES	=	STORE
EIPURCTDNAS	=	UNPRACTISED

ENLDRYACREB = CANDLEBERRY

COMFIT = COMFIT

WPAAPW = PAWPAW

ZQUEERSE = SQUEEZER

CNESLTNIGO = CLINGSTONE

ELSO = SLOE

UTUONIATFLC = FLUCTUATION

IAFTRAA = RATAFIA

RDOCNO = CORDON

BOELDA = ALBEDO

PPIAEGN = GENIPAP

ECERPNRPOP = PEPPERCORN

NOISE POLLUTION

RWLAB	=	BRAWL
UNSIQEETS	=	QUIETNESS
TCOUYR	=	OUTCRY
PLONK	=	PLONK
HPMUT	=	THUMP
SFFELNU	=	SNUFFLE
HLCSA	=	CLASH
OCPRTUINRO	=	CORRUPTION
NKISC	=	SNICK
SINGOUND	=	SOUNDING
WORC	=	CROW
BZZU	=	BUZZ

Puzzle # 42
PACIFIC

RAWATA = TARAWA

AINLCEP = CAPELIN

BILRAOBLD = BROADBILL

OGOERN = OREGON

NALGDCLAAUA = GUADALCANAL

OOCK = COOK

AGMU = GUAM

OHSAVDEHEL = SHOVELHEAD

UGSAR = ARGUS

GDHOFSI = DOGFISH

HOOC = COHO

AIIHTT = TAHITI

Puzzle # 43
CHILDHOOD MEMORIES

OIJRNU = JUNIOR

HIRCEAV = ARCHIVE

KNIHIGTN = THINKING

MIFR = FIRM

SDIIICEALT = IDEALISTIC

KFOL = FOLK

LUTOEBR = TROUBLE

TNCANCTOAEE = CONCATENATE

IEDEVRP = DEPRIVE

AEWKA = AWAKE

FUDRWLENO = WONDERFUL

INHKT = THINK

Puzzle # 44
KIDS PODCASTS

ASSSEESR = REASSESS

GTEINREEC = ENERGETIC

RAWMS = SWARM

OANNTW = WANTON

UOLKOTO = LOOKOUT

CPLRLCEPAAW = CLAPPERCLAW

OETTNANSOTI = OSTENTATION

VERURETO = OVERTURE

BCEKIR = BICKER

EDRLDTO = TODDLER

EGNRRA = RANGER

AWEN = WANE

ABDYN	=	BANDY
DYTEMIA	=	DAYTIME
NEITWRZIE	=	WINTERIZE
PHTDE	=	DEPTH
ADDE	=	DEAD
SOWN	=	SNOW
HTCE	=	ETCH
EGALZD	=	GLAZED
PORVA	=	VAPOR
ISOL	=	SILO
DANSOI	=	ADONIS
ERECNASYS	=	NECESSARY

ABEEFRCYC	=	CYBERCAFE
OCECSNOISN	=	CONCESSION
TIIWSRAE	=	WISTERIA
HUMSATIS	=	TSUSHIMA
YNGA	=	YANG
NHOC	=	CHON
UGATE	=	TAEGU
AEOKR	=	KOREA
NAAPJ	=	JAPAN
TEUG	=	TEGU
TRNEOILA	=	ORIENTAL
UMACTRAHR	=	MACARTHUR

GGLOEG	=	GOGGLE
ATELSR	=	SLATER
EOHNDR	=	HORNED
HREPPOETER	=	TREEHOPPER
GOELOUDDB	=	DOODLEBUG
SPADCI	=	CAPSID
ERIFGBU	=	FIREBUG
TILGBH	=	BLIGHT
RCIEDO	=	COREID
NLEUIEQEVCA	=	EQUIVALENCE
HRATPNEIEM	=	HEMIPTERAN
EPST	=	PEST

Puzzle # 48
SALES SKILLS

MIUAST = AUTISM

SICBA = BASIC

ETHN = THEN

FNAKELR = FLANKER

GARINM = MARGIN

ECPA = PACE

YPKO = POKY

GLIHSUGS = SLUGGISH

EDSPE = SPEED

DEAOHNEB = BONEHEAD

PPPREYE = PEPPERY

NIRAGCH = CHAGRIN

VIOLIN LESSONS

NCHI	=	CHIN
LCSSA	=	CLASS
UETDE	=	ETUDE
NISG	=	SING
OMNAIHRSC	=	HARMONICS
ILNCCI	=	CLINIC
MRACAA	=	MARACA
IRONDSO	=	SORDINO
SIOIINLVT	=	VIOLINIST
EWOBR	=	BOWER
AEBRK	=	BREAK
PSIPTNGO	=	STOPPING

UTOPUT	=	OUTPUT
AELIACBMLP	=	IMPLACABLE
GRAA	=	AGAR
ALCOSELPD	=	SCALLOPED
OTEIYHCD	=	THEODICY
LFLUAEHTH	=	HEALTHFUL
RTOTE	=	TORTE
EEPSRUM	=	SUPREME
FTOS	=	SOFT
RPEHYOBEL	=	HYPERBOLE
FOMA	=	FOAM
UARDCTS	=	CUSTARD

CRAEF = FACER

RTSPO = SPORT

AGHYEWIEHVT = HEAVYWEIGHT

OULF = FOUL

KOPE = POKE

PLEOIRS = SPOILER

MSHLDEUIG = GUMSHIELD

INONEOTNTC = CONTENTION

EASQUR = SQUARE

JDGUE = JUDGE

TKEA = TAKE

DAURG = GUARD

COMSTEU = COSTUME

AKMRRBBCA = BARMBRACK

TONCIDOIN = CONDITION

CTOREH = HECTOR

YNDCA = CANDY

KETNOLSE = SKELETON

RRGFOAA = FARRAGO

LPMEI = IMPEL

YIVIETTFS = FESTIVITY

PAOHOL = HOOPLA

UGLY = UGLY

HSAST = STASH

MAIL

BKLCRERBAY = BLACKBERRY

FRMUFEL = MUFFLER

TNCTMHAEAT = ATTACHMENT

PHPRSOE = SHOPPER

OEEHLNPOGI = PIGEONHOLE

PSERSXE = EXPRESS

YISMEL = SMILEY

YVILDEER = DELIVERY

DNTRECDUIE = UNDIRECTED

RRLUA = RURAL

SREREV = SERVER

EMDAIL = MAILED

Puzzle # 54
KIDS

UEIDOTLESER	=	DELETERIOUS
SLUNEPFLASY	=	PLAYFULNESS
UCKLC	=	CLUCK
AHSDDIF	=	FADDISH
IMUROMEP	=	EMPORIUM
USNA	=	ANUS
LEIABIRLL	=	ILLIBERAL
PCHREAY	=	PREACHY
TSMAOC	=	MASCOT
PSTIL	=	SPLIT
ISRMSE	=	REMISS
FFENEEVCIIT	=	INEFFECTIVE

CAT

UFDRRE	=	FURRED
ASGP	=	GASP
NJUAOKIK	=	KINKAJOU
AKWCLAT	=	CATWALK
EETPRRSEN	=	REPRESENT
AOREPLD	=	LEOPARD
YTTKI	=	KITTY
NBYO	=	BONY
IOCL	=	COIL
ITEAEYNSLSL	=	ESSENTIALLY
SCELKPE	=	SPECKLE
PIWH	=	WHIP

Puzzle # 56
ISLAND HOPPING

ALMKOIO	=	MOLOKAI
OYLCASP	=	CALYPSO
EFLNTOO	=	LOFOTEN
IAGNTUA	=	ANTIGUA
WRARON	=	NARROW
CNLDAIE	=	ICELAND
IANRIITDADN	=	TRINIDADIAN
LEETYMIN	=	MYTILENE
SUHOT	=	SOUTH
TNAAHIIT	=	TAHITIAN
SHOP	=	HOPS
CDOIAINM	=	DOMINICA

Puzzle # 57
CALENDAR

ATUMHZM = THAMMUZ

KPYSEFLC = FLYSPECK

ECKOTD = DOCKET

RAIEMIFR = FRIMAIRE

TEASVH = SHEVAT

RIARAANG = AGRARIAN

MOERSSID = MESSIDOR

MARSK = MARKS

UARJANY = JANUARY

XIEDF = FIXED

FIARE = FERIA

AUILNJ = JULIAN

Puzzle # 58
GREAT MOMENT

OHRU	=	HOUR
KCUD	=	DUCK
ERIW	=	WIRE
TAYEHR	=	HEARTY
TELIJBUA	=	JUBILATE
EIWS	=	WISE
EOHEBNKARRT	=	HEARTBROKEN
PODE	=	DOPE
ABTSL	=	BLAST
OLNEUCSV	=	CONVULSE
GEMIUNDTA	=	MAGNITUDE
GNOMCI	=	COMING

TENSUEISTON = SENTENTIOUS

ADNINISYCTO = SYNDICATION

VNALI = ANVIL

IATMRNOA = ANIMATOR

IBMPL = BLIMP

EYNCSITAD = SYNDICATE

IDEOAITN = IDEATION

YREMANDGERR = GERRYMANDER

POITMEE = EPITOME

WOMANEPR = MANPOWER

DESPSEI = DESPISE

VSILUA = VISUAL

RRIAAGNA = AGRARIAN

INTGILS = LISTING

OPAHTS = POTASH

HARNYBDSU = HUSBANDRY

TRSAO = ROAST

REKAB = BRAKE

OMANID = DOMAIN

RUCUTEL = CULTURE

UINESLTBAAS = SUSTAINABLE

TSKOC = STOCK

BOOT = BOOT

GABOOLYORIG = AGROBIOLOGY

Puzzle # 61
CONCERT

AHCROCNE	=	ENCROACH
KRMA	=	MARK
SEKRIT	=	STRIKE
TSIGRA	=	GRATIS
ATNTDE	=	ATTEND
KRSMEO	=	SMOKER
ITGTENS	=	SETTING
QIEUR	=	QUIRE
NRLVEAIT	=	INTERVAL
ORSONTC	=	CONSORT
UAUIMTODRI	=	AUDITORIUM
EVERDERS	=	RESERVED

Puzzle # 62
OUTDOOR GEAR ACTIVIT

LPAARPE	=	APPAREL
OGORUB	=	BURGOO
ARNEA	=	ARENA
DAANYRL	=	LANYARD
EILANTR	=	LATRINE
BEFOIRN	=	BONFIRE
EWAAYRA	=	AREAWAY
SOATR	=	ROAST
CIRPPLE	=	CRIPPLE
CLNAE	=	CLEAN
RDYA	=	YARD
LCIREHHATSG	=	SEARCHLIGHT

MNAEIDEOC	=	MACEDOINE
EVIDEN	=	ENDIVE
PIOPRAR	=	RORIPPA
RALUUGA	=	ARUGULA
CETUBTONIR	=	CONTRIBUTE
PFIINERTG	=	FINGERTIP
EATANUECCT	=	ACCENTUATE
EHAGCR	=	CHARGE
BCUMCUER	=	CUCUMBER
EULCTTE	=	LETTUCE
OUKILVAS	=	SOUVLAKI
ALZCO	=	COLZA

ROERRAMGMP	=	PROGRAMMER
OECXNEUTI	=	EXECUTION
XEIT	=	EXIT
MYRIRBCEEC	=	CYBERCRIME
CIAHRPG	=	GRAPHIC
MEAULTE	=	EMULATE
TEATSCSE	=	CASSETTE
VNSOII	=	VISION
NADHHEDL	=	HANDHELD
OITMIZPE	=	OPTIMIZE
SUERBTR	=	BURSTER
ENENGI	=	ENGINE

SHNCROCIG	=	SCORCHING
TLSABAL	=	BALLAST
SLWO	=	SLOW
YAEDESWP	=	SPEEDWAY
ELSORS	=	LESSOR
FORO	=	ROOF
IRGP	=	GRIP
RNTE	=	RENT
AOCRNH	=	ANCHOR
BXCAOR	=	BOXCAR
LDDOEA	=	LOADED
ARCSH	=	CRASH

Puzzle # 66
ANIMAL

TTDECAUSRAN = UNCASTRATED

EIRHSF = FISHER

RONRCAI = CARRION

TOAC = COAT

TLNVEA = LEVANT

EBTI = BITE

NALTO = TALON

EAGRES = GREASE

ANHHUC = HAUNCH

LLTAS = STALL

MMYMU = MUMMY

RARIUAVESN = ARENAVIRUS

Puzzle # 67
COOKING

OMSIEANL	=	SEMOLINA
EVLID	=	DEVIL
EMOGTRU	=	GOURMET
HRECNF	=	FRENCH
LSAE	=	SEAL
OEDUNF	=	FONDUE
DODNES	=	SODDEN
OADMNL	=	ALMOND
VOCRKEOO	=	OVERCOOK
ETLCRAE	=	TREACLE
TESW	=	STEW
BROGEA	=	BORAGE

MSTLEETTEN	=	SETTLEMENT
PALTRAI	=	PARTIAL
SPHAE	=	PHASE
OTOR	=	ROOT
MESIUCNS	=	MENISCUS
AAVL	=	LAVA
SICAODAUU	=	AUDACIOUS
OCME	=	COME
ENAW	=	WANE
AREGURL	=	REGULAR
HYESNGU	=	HUYGENS
ELOMSNSO	=	MOONLESS

BSTPKCAO	=	BACKSTOP
EHSTE	=	SHEET
OMLBEI	=	MOBILE
AHTHRE	=	HEARTH
MHEO	=	HOME
ELIXE	=	EXILE
ELIRECTD	=	DERELICT
RDINLEE	=	REDLINE
BBRIE	=	BRIBE
NRCYUREC	=	CURRENCY
UOMNMEC	=	COMMUNE
SDAGAR	=	ASGARD

NAVY

MAARDA = ARMADA

CESREPN = SPENCER

LLLFAOIT = FLOTILLA

AIANRM = AIRMAN

ENAMRI = MARINE

AIORVTA = AVIATOR

SSIREPM = IMPRESS

JIMYM = JIMMY

SALE = SEAL

FRELANEU = FUNEREAL

ALORGOYE = AEROLOGY

MHINICTAS = MACHINIST

Puzzle # 71
CLASSROOM

MISOTRDOFC = DISCOMFORT

HRTIALYI = HILARITY

CLOMHOORSO = SCHOOLROOM

NGAMEMITS = MAGNETISM

EFRKWLIOD = FIELDWORK

ODLDTE = TODDLE

COLKC = CLOCK

UOCSAUR = RAUCOUS

CTROEJP = PROJECT

CCOIMSIRCMO = MICROCOSMIC

OPRPVEA = APPROVE

IATMANNI = MAINTAIN

SAMOCPS = COMPASS

ODOW = WOOD

IYRLTCEEF = ELECTRIFY

IEPERSR = REPRISE

INUAICMS = MUSICIAN

TNIPO = POINT

PPINIG = PIPING

AGRYLN = GNARLY

RMSUT = STRUM

DEAPL = PEDAL

UFIALRG = FIGURAL

NARSEHP = SHARPEN

ITRCETO = COTTIER

NRAIKLNF = FRANKLIN

CCHAE = CACHE

GEEREN = GREENE

EIEPNXCREE = EXPERIENCE

EOLD = LODE

SIWE = WISE

UTPKEA = UPTAKE

ORLYAT = TAYLOR

NPOSO = SNOOP

CTERRA = CARTER

DOHAWR = HOWARD

Puzzle # 74
SIMPLE LIVING

EPODRAYTR = PREDATORY

EFRHCN = FRENCH

NENEIDPNTED = INDEPENDENT

MRANEG = GERMAN

HISTMAIN = ISTHMIAN

EANPTR = PARENT

PLAIEART = PARIETAL

DDPREETA = DEPARTED

MRIT = TRIM

ADBN = BAND

OERV = ROVE

CCANILLI = CLINICAL

Puzzle # 75
INTERIOR DESIGN

SEEERVSLNC   =   CLEVERNESS

TROP   =   PORT

MHATC   =   MATCH

UOFEORSCOPL   =   FLUOROSCOPE

RYFOEWL   =   FLOWERY

EMRIMRT   =   TRIMMER

AYMZ   =   MAZY

NULPDA   =   UPLAND

YEPT   =   TYPE

ODURWSAT   =   OUTWARDS

GTLIANOI   =   INTAGLIO

WOCAOTLRER   =   WATERCOLOR

Puzzle # 76
HOLIDAY

UOCLM	=	LOCUM
NEAEINVLT	=	VALENTINE
ZOMTA	=	MATZO
TSRROE	=	RESORT
SEPEKKEA	=	KEEPSAKE
DUEBSU	=	SUBDUE
RECEOC	=	COERCE
VREEERNEG	=	EVERGREEN
TAEK	=	TAKE
KWAE	=	WAKE
EIRAVIR	=	RIVIERA
OEVSBRE	=	OBSERVE

MOTOCYCLE RACING

NLIENGEUY	=	GENUINELY
HYIDNG	=	DINGHY
NIGTRA	=	RATING
TOUBOKDS	=	STUDBOOK
HAKC	=	HACK
NOREBK	=	BROKEN
RSESP	=	PRESS
BMROKKAEO	=	BOOKMAKER
CRSUTNTCORO	=	CONSTRUCTOR
KLSI	=	SILK
EEHLVCI	=	VEHICLE
OKOIEB	=	BOOKIE

NISAOOACITS	=	ASSOCIATION
PITACVYIT	=	CAPTIVITY
FDLEI	=	FIELD
EITDEEMFLN	=	DEFILEMENT
UNCEALP	=	CLEANUP
IOSENRTRIAP	=	RESPIRATION
UNROUSRD	=	SURROUND
TOIALGENNC	=	CONGENITAL
ICEMANEB	=	AMBIENCE
ALITHYLCE	=	ETHICALLY
LRUAMISTO	=	SIMULATOR
TLESEIR	=	STERILE

BEAUTY

CBNEIAT	=	CABINET
SIGN	=	SING
ENGAETL	=	ELEGANT
EIDSDPNL	=	SPLENDID
MOCICTSE	=	COSMETIC
OLMARGU	=	GLAMOUR
FLEE	=	FEEL
SPERO	=	PROSE
PGTEAAN	=	PAGEANT
ROLGY	=	GLORY
TNCTENTASO	=	CONTESTANT
ADUOTWR	=	OUTWARD

MASH = SHAM

RUCCIS = CIRCUS

CTUCLO = OCCULT

NHEOTIIIXB = EXHIBITION

IANRT = TRAIN

LGNAEW = WANGLE

ONMEG = GNOME

IOSBILMAD = DIABOLISM

JOSNHNO = JOHNSON

TSAMIO = TAOISM

TRFCA = CRAFT

DDEGO = DODGE

Puzzle # 81
BALLOON

DHEATEHIGDL	=	LIGHTHEADED
RBSTU	=	BURST
GAASNBD	=	SANDBAG
IGTILPNFU	=	UPLIFTING
IENFRTS	=	SNIFTER
UCSAFRE	=	SURFACE
LTFI	=	LIFT
DNTMIENYI	=	INDEMNITY
IURTDG	=	TURGID
KALE	=	LEAK
LOKYLJI	=	KILLJOY
LENIATF	=	INFLATE

Puzzle # 82
CHINA

NTIAINJ	=	TIANJIN
AAKRAOKMR	=	KARAKORAM
KIATN	=	TAKIN
NGNGTKWUA	=	KWANGTUNG
IAHJKISRNI	=	JINRIKISHA
NNUAH	=	HUNAN
NCMAUH	=	MANCHU
TMJUCAN	=	MUNTJAC
IWWLAEWLOR	=	WILLOWWARE
LUANIR	=	URINAL
ICER	=	RICE
GNUS	=	SUNG

NMNWOI	=	MINNOW
SALPOLC	=	SCALLOP
DIOPNCIYR	=	CYPRINOID
EIHFLIKS	=	FISHLIKE
FDSPNIHO	=	FISHPOND
CKOO	=	COOK
ALSCE	=	SCALE
FIPSHAERS	=	SPEARFISH
SLAHO	=	SHOAL
HFOSRBAI	=	BOARFISH
WFAELIE	=	ALEWIFE
CCDYOLI	=	CYCLOID

DGIEU	=	GUIDE
GORIBNH	=	BIGHORN
HRAKCATD	=	HARDTACK
BVINLISIE	=	INVISIBLE
TEBUT	=	BUTTE
SMJAAA	=	SAJAMA
ACCSAUUS	=	CAUCASUS
NTLENU	=	TUNNEL
ATOMRNTANE	=	TRAMONTANE
TLWRESHI	=	WHISTLER
KAERB	=	BAKER
MUOTASEN	=	SEAMOUNT

OIUNDCGRFE = CONFIGURED

ELFRTTU = FLUTTER

AQNBUET = BANQUET

TDIAM = ADMIT

LKOO = LOOK

ARBW = BRAW

CIOCEIND = COINCIDE

SURPEDLMEO = SUPERMODEL

AERNTTP = PATTERN

GDFELNEWAN = NEWFANGLED

YNURAW = RUNWAY

EDAUNTD = UNDATED

Puzzle # 86
BATHROOM

YPOTT	=	POTTY
WSBSAAHIN	=	WASHBASIN
MATPENRTA	=	APARTMENT
AYRBNI	=	BINARY
NISK	=	SINK
STHEITR	=	SHITTER
VTSOE	=	STOVE
ELRZVEBAI	=	VERBALIZE
EEDENNDNTIP	=	INDEPENDENT
EVRIPETEIT	=	REPETITIVE
NPUGREL	=	PLUNGER
OLIZEBMMII	=	IMMOBILIZE

TRAVEL

IROBT	=	ORBIT
CCHTA	=	CATCH
EPLACUS	=	CAPSULE
RIESVCE	=	SERVICE
BOBM	=	BOMB
OSAENS	=	SEASON
AIPRRE	=	REPAIR
KRSEIT	=	STRIKE
TIPR	=	TRIP
URCEIRO	=	COURIER
TRENREY	=	REENTRY
ORTLOAC	=	LOCATOR

TELEVISION

RSESIE	=	SERIES
LREASI	=	SERIAL
IKLN	=	LINK
IUSALV	=	VISUAL
LYAIDSP	=	DISPLAY
CEMCRDOAR	=	CAMCORDER
FONRT	=	FRONT
TPRERROE	=	REPORTER
NOOWRSME	=	NEWSROOM
NECEPRITO	=	RECEPTION
NIATRG	=	RATING
MOURF	=	FORUM

EMSGRNEES	=	MESSENGER
LTVO	=	VOLT
HENEDUGRACR	=	UNDERCHARGE
BXEOIC	=	ICEBOX
MSBEASLE	=	ASSEMBLE
ECHOATD	=	CATHODE
FREAIMN	=	FIREMAN
OALRP	=	POLAR
EILCALRCTE	=	ELECTRICAL
HGAERDC	=	CHARGED
NIFEFDERINT	=	INDIFFERENT
EPMGRAAE	=	AMPERAGE

Puzzle # 90
ANTI AGING

UKNP	=	PUNK
EDRUS	=	DRUSE
REEGSSR	=	REGRESS
RZTEFAINEE	=	ANTIFREEZE
SETOCORNI	=	CORTISONE
BTIAICIONT	=	ANTIBIOTIC
ALLTIFP	=	PITFALL
MOSTOH	=	SMOOTH
TSITRIHRA	=	ARTHRITIS
IANT	=	ANTI
RGOEU	=	ROGUE
NFIOUERBP	=	IBUPROFEN

TEAT	=	TEAT
ATMOUN	=	AMOUNT
XPACEIOTNLE	=	EXCEPTIONAL
CYEWARA	=	RACEWAY
CDDOBRAAR	=	CARDBOARD
VERSESCNLE	=	CLEVERNESS
KNIGONW	=	KNOWING
LTISSWE	=	WITLESS
IALYWCUES	=	SLUICEWAY
OCUKOC	=	CUCKOO
NIOISV	=	VISION
NTHAMTDEOU	=	MUTTONHEAD

NERATK	=	TANKER
EDISLE	=	DIESEL
LDOMA	=	MODAL
AGLONDO	=	GONDOLA
LIEN	=	LINE
RKRCTUE	=	TRUCKER
ITHMENSP	=	SHIPMENT
SMPDRETU	=	DUMPSTER
ETARRB	=	BARTER
PCOH	=	CHOP
ECKER	=	CREEK
HARTWDROOY	=	ROADWORTHY

OFFICE

CAPOIITTFEN	=	PONTIFICATE
RHNYAROO	=	HONORARY
PDAOT	=	ADOPT
SPDHHIEA	=	HEADSHIP
CSRJYITIAU	=	JUSTICIARY
SAWRDNPEIH	=	WARDENSHIP
ITNVSE	=	INVEST
HBNEC	=	BENCH
NAUHTEGSO	=	SHOGUNATE
DSOMIITAPLT	=	DIPLOMATIST
PPAIANECL	=	APPLIANCE
ASCK	=	SACK

Puzzle # 94
WORKING

ELVEA	=	LEAVE
OAITNREPVEI	=	INOPERATIVE
NSITAR	=	STRAIN
GABREE	=	BARGEE
CETSRE	=	SECRET
RANK	=	NARK
ESOTIMUCUL	=	METICULOUS
ITONTDAE	=	ANTIDOTE
FASNAREGI	=	SEAFARING
EROC	=	CORE
WKRREO	=	WORKER
NBIDBO	=	DOBBIN

CAREER

PIEPYU = YUPPIE

RTNOFUE = FORTUNE

AGLGINFG = FLAGGING

CAME = ACME

RALET = LATER

RESVDIA = ADVISER

REITER = RETIRE

ULAIIDCJR = JURIDICAL

RNYJUI = INJURY

EMETNTEIRR = RETIREMENT

ICATVOON = VOCATION

OHEW = HOWE

CPLAAA = ALPACA

VAEWE = WEAVE

XBDBANO = BANDBOX

RIETTAEG = AIGRETTE

RDWLA = DRAWL

ANOLLOB = BALLOON

KINT = KNIT

RLTNCCAEUE = RELUCTANCE

NHAFOMF = HOFFMAN

CKOLB = BLOCK

OLBGEI = OBLIGE

SDAAHLLTN = HALLSTAND

ESTATE PLANNING

EHITNEQCU = TECHNIQUE

AENAWOLLC = ALLOWANCE

ONJIERUT = JOINTURE

ECSLO = CLOSE

ICSNYD = SYNDIC

ITTRENSE = INTEREST

BORNYA = BARONY

INDAOM = DOMAIN

HOISOGNT = SHOOTING

TRHIREO = HERITOR

TERTEEMBTN = BETTERMENT

GINIXF = FIXING

Puzzle # 98
FILM MAKING

UYDTSR	=	STURDY
LERLOR	=	ROLLER
CUARNFUTEAM	=	MANUFACTURE
DIGANWD	=	WADDING
LNSUMAOJRI	=	JOURNALISM
AEGMI	=	IMAGE
ISNCNSNALEO	=	NONSENSICAL
SENVRTATII	=	TRANSITIVE
ORLIPFAEBT	=	PROFITABLE
LPIB	=	BLIP
RAKTC	=	TRACK
TIDADICC	=	DIDACTIC

NNOFROTEA	=	AFTERNOON
ASREPIT	=	TRAIPSE
UNSH	=	SHUN
NTCTNEGOIN	=	CONTINGENT
ATRRNUSATE	=	RESTAURANT
PILF	=	FLIP
ANMDOR	=	RANDOM
YAROTAHWW	=	THROWAWAY
OSNG	=	SNOG
HTEOPCPRI	=	PROPHETIC
RTSPO	=	SPORT
REITSK	=	STRIKE

Puzzle # 100
HOSPITAL

IAILPEZHTOS   =   HOSPITALIZE

SYROANAITT   =   STATIONARY

UEATRNAQIN   =   QUARANTINE

ITSIACPTNE   =   ANTISEPTIC

EMTAIN   =   INMATE

IGENDDB   =   BEDDING

RATRES   =   ARREST

RXENTE   =   EXTERN

IREECVGRA   =   CAREGIVER

OIOSVARBNTE   =   OBSERVATION

AEATRLNM   =   MATERNAL

ERCA   =   RACE